Fresh & Easy
Family Meals

Gooseberry Patch

An imprint of Globe Pequot
246 Goose Lane
Guilford, CT 06437

www.gooseberrypatch.com

1•800•854•6673

Copyright 2015, Gooseberry Patch 978-1-62093-180-6

Do you have a tried & true recipe...

tip, craft or memory that you'd like to see featured in
a **Gooseberry Patch** cookbook? Visit our website at
www.gooseberrypatch.com and follow the
easy steps to submit your favorite family recipe.
Or send them to us at:

Gooseberry Patch
PO Box 812
Columbus, OH 43216-0812

Don't forget to include the number of servings your recipe makes,
plus your name, address, phone number and email address. If we
select your recipe, your name will appear right along with it...
and you'll receive a **FREE** copy of the book!

CONTENTS

Dedication

To everyone who loves sharing good home-cooked food with family & friends.

Appreciation

Many thanks to everyone who shared their most delicious family recipes with us.

Breakfasts
to Start the Day Right

Denver Oven Omelet

Charlene McCain
Bakersfield, CA

Delicious and easy! I have taken this simple dish to many breakfast potlucks, since it bakes while I get ready for work. My family even enjoys it on Christmas morning after we've opened our presents.

8 eggs, beaten
1/2 c. half-and-half
1 c. shredded Cheddar cheese
1 c. cooked ham, chopped

1/4 c. green pepper, chopped
1/4 c. onion, finely chopped
salt and pepper to taste

In a large bowl, whisk eggs and half-and-half until light and fluffy. Stir in remaining ingredients. Pour into a greased 9"x9" baking pan. Bake, uncovered, at 400 degrees for 25 minutes, or until set and golden. Serves 4.

Take it easy at breakfast time. The night before, whisk eggs for scrambling, chop veggies for omelets and tuck them in the refrigerator. Dry ingredients for muffins or waffles can be mixed up in advance too. In the morning, you'll be able to serve up breakfast with a minimum of fuss.

Best Blueberry Muffins

Sue Troth
Alberta, Canada

I looked for a long time for a blueberry muffin recipe that was soft and cake-like. Since I found this one, I haven't looked back. Use the best margarine you can find...you won't be sorry!

2 c. fresh blueberries
2-1/4 c. all-purpose flour,
    divided
4 t. baking powder
1 t. salt

1/4 c. margarine
1-1/2 c. sugar
2 eggs, beaten
1 t. vanilla extract
1 c. 2% milk

Sprinkle blueberries with 1/4 cup flour and fold gently until coated; set aside. In a separate bowl, combine remaining flour, baking powder and salt; mix well. In another bowl, blend margarine and sugar well. In a cup, whisk together eggs and vanilla; add to margarine mixture and stir well. Add flour mixture and milk alternately to margarine mixture; mix well. Add blueberries and mix gently. Fill 24 greased muffin cups 2/3 full. Bake at 375 degrees for 20 to 25 minutes, until lightly golden. Makes 2 dozen.

A baker's secret! Grease muffin cups on the bottoms and just halfway up the sides. Muffins will bake up nicely puffed on top.

Cheesy Egg & Ham Skillet

Beckie Apple
Grannis, AR

This is a great low-carb dish. My husband and I love it even when we aren't counting carbs! Serve it for breakfast, brunch or even a supper meal with a fresh salad.

3 c. shredded Cheddar cheese, divided
2 T. oil
1/4 c. onion, diced

2 T. green pepper, diced
1 c. cooked ham, diced
5 eggs
salt and pepper to taste

Spray a non-stick skillet well with olive or canola oil non-stick spray. Heat skillet over medium heat. Evenly spread 2 cups cheese to cover the bottom of skillet. Cover and cook over medium heat about 3 minutes, until cheese forms a crust. To a separate skillet, add oil, onion, pepper and ham. Sauté over medium heat until onion and pepper are tender; set aside. Break eggs over cheese crust in first skillet; lightly season with salt and pepper. Pierce egg yolks with a fork so that yolks will spread over the cheese. Cover skillet and continue cooking over medium heat for 3 minutes. Evenly spoon onion mixture over eggs; sprinkle with remaining cheese. Cover skillet; remove from heat and let stand for 3 to 4 minutes. With a spatula, loosen edges of crust and slide onto a large serving plate. Cut into wedges. Makes 4 to 6 servings.

Eggs and potatoes are tasty with catsup, but to really wake everyone up at breakfast time, add some spicy salsa or hot pepper sauce.

Ham Quiche Cups

Kristi Likes
Stonington, IL

On busy mornings, it's so handy to have some of these little gems tucked in the freezer, ready to reheat. They're very easy to change up by using sausage instead of ham and adding your favorite cheese.

1 T. butter
1 c. frozen diced onion and
    peppers seasoning blend
4 slices cooked deli ham,
    chopped

6 eggs, beaten
1/2 t. Italian seasoning
pepper to taste
1 c. shredded mozzarella cheese

Melt butter in a skillet over medium heat. Add onion blend and cook until vegetables are tender, about 4 minutes. Add ham and cook another minute. Remove skillet from stove; let stand for 5 to 10 minutes. Meanwhile, preheat oven to 350 degrees. In a bowl, whisk together eggs and seasonings; mix in cheese. Add onion mixture and stir until combined. Ladle into 12 greased muffin cups, 2 tablespoons per cup. Bake at 350 degrees for about 20 minutes, until eggs are set. Serve immediately, or wrap individually and place in plastic zipping bags. May keep refrigerated up to 2 days or frozen for one month. Warm in microwave. Makes one dozen muffins.

Best tip ever for success in the kitchen! Read the recipe the whole way through and make sure you have everything you'll need before you start cooking.

Best Buttermilk Apple Pie Pancakes

Marti Cooper
Lewisville, TX

I'm trying to make breakfast and pancakes healthier so I added apples to the pancake batter. Not only is it a little more healthy, but these are the best pancakes I've ever had!

2 c. all-purpose flour
3 T. sugar
2 t. baking powder
1 t. baking soda
1/2 t. cinnamon
1/2 t. salt
21-oz. can apple pie filling,
    divided

2 eggs, lightly beaten
2-1/2 to 3 c. buttermilk
2 to 3 T. butter
Garnish: whipped cream,
    cinnamon

In a large bowl, whisk together flour, sugar, baking powder, baking soda, cinnamon and salt. Measure out one cup pie filling and dice any large pieces of apple. Add this pie filling to flour mixture along with eggs and 2-1/2 cups buttermilk. Stir well; batter will be lumpy. Add remaining buttermilk as needed. Heat a griddle over medium heat; test for readiness by putting a few drops of water on griddle. When water bounces or spatters, it is ready. Melt one teaspoon butter onto griddle; add batter by 1/2 cupfuls. Cook until pancakes start to form bubbles on top; turn over and cook other side. Add more butter as needed. To serve, top each pancake with remaining pie filling, a dollop of whipped cream and a dash of cinnamon. Makes 8 to 10 pancakes.

Making pancakes for a crowd? Stack them on a plate and slide into a 175-degree oven. They'll stay warm until serving time.

Simple Homemade Pancakes

Cynthia Johnson
Verona, WI

These egg-free pancakes are my kids' favorite Sunday morning treat!

1 c. all-purpose flour
2 T. sugar
2 t. baking powder
2 T. butter

1/2 c. applesauce
1-1/4 c. milk
1/4 t. cinnamon

Mix flour, sugar and baking powder in a small bowl. Place butter in a large microwave-safe bowl; microwave for 30 seconds, until butter melts. Add applesauce, milk and cinnamon to butter and stir. Gradually stir flour mixture into butter mixture. Ladle batter by 1/2 cupfuls onto a greased non-stick griddle over medium heat. Cook until bubbles appear on edges of pancakes. Turn over; cook until golden on other side. Makes about 12 thin pancakes.

Nauvoo Syrup for Pancakes & Waffles

Jill Ball
Highland, UT

This recipe has been passed down from generation to generation. It comes from a time before my great-great-great grandmother loaded her family into a small wagon and headed west.

3/4 c. sugar
1/2 c. buttermilk
1/2 c. butter, sliced

1 t. vanilla extract
1 t. baking soda

Combine sugar, buttermilk and butter in a medium saucepan. Cook, stirring often, over medium-low heat until butter is melted and sugar is dissolved. Remove from heat; carefully stir in vanilla and baking soda. Syrup will rise to top of pan as baking soda is added. Serve warm over pancakes or waffles. Makes 12 servings.

Cut up pancakes in a jiffy using a pizza cutter.

Veggie Egg Muffins

Courtney Stultz
Columbus, KS

As a busy mom, mornings are crazy for me. I love finding shortcuts anywhere I can and these healthy muffins are perfect. They are loaded with veggies for great nutrition. They freeze well too!

18 eggs or egg white equivalent, beaten
6-oz. container plain yogurt or 3/4 c. milk
1 t. dried sage
1 t. sea salt
1/2 t. pepper
1 c. broccoli, finely chopped
1/2 c. cauliflower, finely chopped
1/2 c. carrots, peeled and finely chopped
1 to 2 c. shredded Cheddar cheese
Garnish: sour cream, salsa, catsup or sriracha sauce

Combine all ingredients except garnish in a large bowl; whisk until blended. Pour into 20 ungreased muffin cups, filling 2/3 full. Bake at 375 degrees for about 20 to 25 minutes, until eggs are set and golden. Garnish as desired. To freeze, let muffins cool completely. Store in a plastic freezer bag or container for up to 3 months. Reheat in microwave or oven. Makes 20 muffins.

Keep frozen chopped onions, peppers and other veggies on hand. They'll thaw quickly so you can assemble a recipe in a snap...no peeling, chopping or dicing needed!

Sausage Egg Muffins

Jewel Sharpe
Raleigh, NC

Easiest breakfast ever!

1 lb. ground pork breakfast
   sausage
1 c. biscuit baking mix

4 eggs, beaten
1 c. sharp shredded Cheddar
   cheese

In a skillet over medium-high heat, cook and crumble sausage until browned. Drain well; transfer sausage to a large bowl. Add biscuit mix, eggs and cheese; stir well. Spoon mixture into lightly greased muffin cups, filling 2/3 full. Bake at 350 degrees for 20 minutes, or until set and lightly golden. Serve warm. Makes one dozen muffins.

Poached eggs for a crowd! For each egg, add one tablespoon water to a muffin cup. Break an egg directly into each cup. Bake at 350 degrees, 11 to 13 minutes for runny yolks, a bit longer for firmer yolks. Remove from oven and let stand for one minute, then gently remove eggs with a slotted spoon.

Honey Walnut Granola

Elizabeth McCord
Bartlett, TN

This recipe is one that I came up with after searching for the perfect granola recipe. It's perfect for breakfast or as a snack. I especially enjoy it topped with vanilla yogurt and fresh blueberries.

3 c. rolled oats, uncooked
3/4 c. chopped walnuts
6 to 8 T. pure maple syrup or
    pancake syrup

6 to 7 T. honey
1/4 c. water
1/4 c. olive oil
3/4 T. vanilla extract

In a large bowl, combine all ingredients together and mix well. Spread out on a greased baking sheet. Bake at 325 degrees for 20 minutes. Remove from oven and stir gently. Bake for another 8 to 10 minutes, or a little longer if a crunchier texture is preferred. Remove from oven and let granola cool completely on baking sheet. Break up and store in a plastic zipping bag or an airtight container. Makes 12 to 16 servings.

Save the plastic liners when you toss out empty cereal boxes. They're perfect for storing homemade granola and snack mixes.

Oat Bran Muffins

Sandy Barnhart
Sapulpa, OK

These muffins are yummy anytime, not just for breakfast!
When I have ripe bananas and don't want to make
banana bread or cake, this is my go-to recipe.

1 c. brown sugar, packed
1 egg, lightly beaten
1 c. bananas, mashed,
   or applesauce
1/2 c. oil
1 t. vanilla extract
1 c. oat bran

1 c. whole-wheat flour or
   all-purpose flour
1 t. baking powder
1/4 t. salt
1/2 c. raisins, sunflower seed
   kernels or chopped walnuts

Combine all ingredients in a large bowl; mix well. Spoon batter into 12 greased or paper-lined muffin cups, filling 2/3 full. Bake at 350 degrees for 25 minutes, or until set; don't overbake. Makes one dozen muffins.

If you love freshly baked muffins, pick up a set of stackable, reusable silicone baking cups. They come in lots of bright colors and are also handy for other purposes like serving mini portions of fruit, nuts or chips.

Creamy Egg Bake

JoAnn

Everyone gets their own little breakfast portion...just add some hot buttered toast!

2 t. butter, softened	salt and pepper to taste
3 T. whipping cream	4 t. fresh chives, minced
8 eggs	4 t. grated Parmesan cheese

Spread butter inside 4 ramekins or custard cups. Divide cream evenly among ramekins. Crack 2 eggs into each ramekin, keeping yolks unbroken. Season with salt and pepper; sprinkle with chives and cheese. Set ramekins on a baking sheet. Bake at 325 degrees for 12 to 15 minutes, until egg whites have set and yolks are still soft. Remove from oven. Let stand for a few minutes before serving. Makes 4 servings.

Toad in a Hole, Egg in a Nest...whatever the name, kids love 'em and they're so easy to fix. Cut out the center of a slice of bread with a small cookie cutter. Add the bread to a buttered skillet over medium heat and break an egg into the hole. Cook until golden on the bottom, turn over with a spatula and cook until the egg is set as you like.

Clean-Out-the-Fridge Frittata

Cindy Kemp
Lake Jackson, TX

When I found a recipe for frittata, I was inspired by some leftovers in the fridge. The ingredients are only limited by your imagination... you'll hardly know they are leftovers! This makes a wonderful "breakfast for dinner" meal too. It is delicious and filling on its own, even better with hashbrowns or grits.

6 eggs
1/2 c. water
1/4 to 1/2 c. cooked meats,
    cut into bite-size pieces
1/4 to 1/2 c. cooked vegetables,
    cut into bite-size pieces

1/4 c. salsa
Optional: 1/4 c. sliced
    mushrooms
salt and pepper to taste
1 c. shredded Cheddar or
    mozzarella cheese, divided

In a large bowl, whisk eggs until well beaten. Add water and whisk well. Add remaining ingredients except cheese. Mix well and stir in 1/2 cup cheese. Pour mixture into a cast-iron skillet or a one-quart casserole dish that has been sprayed with non-stick vegetable spray. Top with remaining cheese. Bake, uncovered, at 400 degrees for about 30 to 40 minutes, until center is set. Makes 6 to 8 servings.

When chopping veggies, set the cutting board on a damp kitchen towel and it won't slip. Works with mixing bowls when you're stirring up batter too.

Nested Eggs

Courtney Stultz
Columbus, KS

We love one-dish meals as they make prep and clean-up so easy. We also love a tasty, hearty breakfast (or dinner!) that keeps us going throughout the day. This recipe is both, and it's easily doubled.

2 T. coconut oil or butter
3 oz. ground pork breakfast
    sausage
2 potatoes, peeled and shredded
2 c. fresh spinach, chopped

1 t. sea salt
1/2 t. pepper
1/2 t. dried sage
3 to 4 eggs

In a cast-iron skillet, melt coconut oil or butter over medium heat. Add sausage and cook until browned. Remove sausage from skillet to a plate; set aside. Add potatoes to drippings in skillet. Sauté over medium heat, stirring occasionally, for about 10 minutes, until softened. Spread potatoes over bottom of skillet for the "nest." Top with sausage and spinach; sprinkle with seasonings. Crack eggs over top of mixture; sprinkle with additional pepper, if desired. Bake, uncovered, at 375 degrees for about 20 minutes, until eggs are cooked through. Serves 2.

Cookie cutters make breakfast a treat...use them to cut out biscuits, shape pancakes or cut shapes from the centers of French toast. Use mini cutters to make the sweetest pats of butter.

Breakfasts *to Start the Day Right*

Microwaved Scrambled Eggs

Carrie Kelderman
Pella, IA

Got a hungry family? This is a quick recipe for making a large portion of scrambled eggs! It's terrific when you don't want to spend your time hovering over the stove.

1/4 c. butter, sliced
8 eggs, beaten
1/4 c. milk

1/4 c. grated Parmesan cheese
1/2 t. salt

Place butter in a large microwave-safe bowl. Microwave on high until butter melts. Meanwhile, in a separate bowl, whisk together remaining ingredients; add to butter and beat well. Microwave on high until eggs are set but slightly moist, 3 to 4 minutes. Remove from microwave. Cover and let stand until eggs are firm, 2 to 3 minutes. If eggs are still not set, return to microwave for 30 seconds. Makes 6 to 8 servings.

Scrambled Egg in a Cup

Lisa Sett
Thousand Oaks, CA

This is my favorite "breakfast on the go" before I go to the gym. Comes out perfect every time! Easy for older kids to make for themselves...try it on an English muffin.

1 egg
salt and pepper to taste
2 T. fresh spinach, chopped

Garnish: 1 to 2 t. shredded cheese, salsa, sliced green onion

Beat egg, salt and pepper well in a greased microwave-safe mug; add spinach. Microwave on high for one minute. Garnish as desired and serve from mug. Serves one.

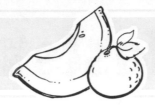

Favorite Banana Waffles

Phyl Broich-Wessling
Garner, IA

Try these tender waffles for breakfast or a snack, topped with a sprinkling of mini chocolate chips and your favorite toasted nuts or a dollop of whipped cream and sliced fresh strawberries.

1-1/3 c. all-purpose flour
1/2 t. salt
2 t. baking powder
2 eggs, separated
1 T. sugar

1/4 c. butter, melted and
   slightly cooled
1 c. milk
1 ripe banana, mashed

In a large bowl, mix flour, salt and baking powder together. In a small bowl, beat egg yolks until light and foamy; stir in sugar and butter. Add milk to egg yolk mixture alternately with flour mixture. Blend in banana; set aside. With an electric mixer on high speed, beat egg whites until stiff peaks form; fold into batter. Drop batter by 1/2 cupfuls onto a lightly greased hot waffle iron. Bake according to manufacturer's directions. Makes 6 waffles.

Extra waffles and pancakes can be frozen separately
in plastic freezer bags for up to a month. Reheat them
in a toaster for a quick breakfast.

Southern Cornmeal Waffles

Lori Ritchey
Denver, PA

I live in the northeast and occasionally we get a hankering for something southern. This waffle recipe is easy and delicious...perfect with country ham.

3/4 c. yellow cornmeal
2 T. all-purpose flour
1 t. sugar
1/2 t. baking powder
1/4 t. baking soda

1/4 t. salt
1 egg, beaten
1 c. milk
1/4 c. oil
2 t. lemon juice

In a bowl, mix together cornmeal, flour, sugar, baking powder, baking soda and salt. Stir in remaining ingredients. Drop batter by 1/2 cupfuls onto a lightly greased hot waffle iron. Bake according to manufacturer's directions. Makes 4 to 6 waffles.

A jar of honey is a sweet addition to the breakfast table
to enjoy on hot toast or pancakes or drizzle into hot tea.
If the honey has crystallized, simply set the jar in a pan of
hot water. After a few minutes, it will be ready to use again.

Anne's Blueberry Pancakes

Anne Alesauskas
Minocqua, WI

*I just love breakfast for dinner and these pancakes are
a favorite of mine. My oldest, Andrew, likes to make syrup in
the spring and pure Wisconsin maple syrup is such a treat!*

1-1/2 c. all-purpose flour
3 T. sugar
1 T. baking powder
1/4 t. salt
2 eggs, beaten

1-1/4 c. milk
1/2 t. vanilla extract
2 c. blueberries
Garnish: butter, pure maple
   syrup

In a large bowl, combine all ingredients except blueberries and garnish.
Stir until just a few lumps remain. Let batter stand for a few minutes.
Heat a lightly greased griddle over medium-high heat. Drop batter onto
griddle by 1/3 cupfuls. Scatter blueberries over batter. Cook until
golden on the bottom and bubbles form on top. Flip over and cook
until done on the other side, being careful not to burn the blueberries.
Serve with butter and maple syrup. Makes about one dozen pancakes.

Breakfast sliders! Whip up your favorite pancake batter and
make silver dollar–size pancakes. Sandwich them together
with slices of heat & serve sausage. Serve with maple
syrup on the side for dipping...yum!

Krunchy Krispies Bacon

Pam Massey
Marshall, AR

Just a little country trick to make the same old thing taste a little different...adds a little extra crunch.

12 slices bacon, halved   1/2 c. all-purpose flour

Roll bacon slices in flour, shaking off any excess flour. Arrange bacon on an aluminum foil-lined baking sheet. Bake at 375 degrees until bacon is crisp, about 12 to 15 minutes depending on thickness of bacon. Drain on paper towels before serving. Makes 6 servings.

Honey-Cinnamon Pancake Syrup

Becky Hall
Belton, MO

My family loves to pour on the syrup when eating pancakes, waffles or French toast. This simple recipe is yummy but not so sugary.

1 c. water   1/8 t. orange zest
1 c. honey   1/8 t. lemon zest
1 t. cinnamon

Combine all ingredients in a small saucepan over medium heat. Bring to a boil; reduce heat to low. Simmer, uncovered, for about 30 minutes, stirring often. Serve warm. Makes 4 servings.

When measuring sticky ingredients like honey or peanut butter, spray the measuring cup with non-stick vegetable spray first. The contents will slip right out and you'll get a more accurate measurement.

Sunday Morning Waffles

Eleanor Dionne
Beverly, MA

*These tasty waffles have been a longtime favorite for leisurely
Sunday breakfasts, when we have more time to enjoy
making and eating them together.*

1 c. wheat germ
3/4 c. whole-wheat flour
1/2 c. unbleached all-purpose
   flour
1 T. baking powder
1/2 t. salt

2 eggs, beaten
1 c. plain yogurt
1 c. milk
1/3 c. canola oil
2 to 4 T. pure maple syrup

In a medium bowl, combine wheat germ, flours, baking powder and
salt; set aside. In a large bowl, beat together remaining ingredients.
Add flour mixture to egg mixture and stir until smooth. Let stand for
a few minutes. Drop batter by 1/2 cupfuls onto a lightly greased hot
waffle iron. Bake according to manufacturer's directions. Makes 4 to
6 waffles.

Watch for old-fashioned syrup or cream pitchers at tag sales...
set out a variety of sweet toppings like flavored syrups
and honey for fluffy pancakes and waffles.

Breakfasts *to Start the Day Right*

Apple-Sausage Pancakes

Heather Nagel
Cleveland, OH

I first had these at my friend Beth's house for brunch. They were so good! A couple years later at my bridal shower, I was so happy to find this recipe taped to the griddle she bought me as a gift.

1/2 lb. ground pork breakfast
   sausage
1 egg, beaten
1 c. pancake mix

2/3 c. oil
1/2 t. cinnamon
1/2 c. apple, cored and shredded

Brown sausage in a skillet over medium heat; drain. Meanwhile, in a bowl, mix together egg, pancake mix, oil and cinnamon. Fold in sausage and apple. Drop batter by 1/2 cupfuls onto a hot greased griddle. Cook until golden on both sides. Serve with Apple Syrup. Makes one dozen pancakes.

Apple Syrup:

1 c. apple cider or apple juice
1/2 c. sugar
3 T. butter, sliced

1 T. cornstarch
1 T. lemon juice
1/8 t. pumpkin pie spice

Combine all ingredients in a saucepan over medium-high heat. Stir well and bring to a boil. Reduce heat to low; keep warm until ready to serve.

When breaking eggs, if part of a broken eggshell gets into
the bowl, just dip in half of an already-broken eggshell.
The broken bit will grab onto it like a magnet.

Chilly-Morning Coffee Cake

Carol Brownridge
Ontario, Canada

Whenever the weather starts to get cool, I always make coffee cake for Saturday morning breakfast. It's great because if we don't finish it for breakfast, we can nibble on it throughout the day. It never lasts more than a day in our house!

1-1/2 c. all-purpose flour
3/4 c. sugar
1-1/2 t. baking powder
1/2 t. salt
1/3 c. shortening

1 egg
1/2 c. milk
1/2 t. vanilla extract
2 T. butter, melted

In a large bowl, mix together flour, sugar, baking powder and salt. Cut in shortening to the size of small peas, using a pastry blender or 2 table knives. In a separate bowl, beat egg; whisk in milk and vanilla. Add egg mixture to flour mixture. Stir carefully until just blended; do not overmix. Pour batter into a greased and floured 9"x9" baking pan and spread evenly. Drizzle with melted butter. Sprinkle Crumb Topping over butter. Bake at 425 degrees for 15 to 20 minutes. Cut into squares. Makes 9 servings.

Crumb Topping:

1/2 c. brown sugar, packed
2 T. all-purpose flour

1 t. cinnamon

In a bowl, mix together all ingredients.

Deliver a tray of your favorite breakfast goodies to the teachers' lounge at school...it's sure to be appreciated!

Breakfasts *to Start the Day Right*

Blueberry Breakfast Soup

Teresa Eller
Tonganoxie, KS

I make this fruity oatmeal "soup" almost every morning. I began taking it on the go when I needed to get to work early. My travel mug keeps it hot until I am ready to eat it.

1 c. water
1/4 c. old-fashioned oats, uncooked
1/4 c. chopped walnuts

1/2 c. fresh or frozen blueberries
1/2 t. cinnamon
4 t. honey

In a small saucepan over medium heat, bring water to a boil. Stir in oats, walnuts, blueberries and cinnamon. Cook for 3 minutes, stirring occasionally. Drizzle with honey. Serve immediately, or spoon into a coffee travel mug. Serves one.

Write it on your heart that every day
is the best day of the year.
– Ralph Waldo Emerson

Sugar–Free Granola

Elizabeth Quigley
League City, TX

I've been cutting sugar from my diet due to health issues,
but I wanted something sweet to sprinkle on top of my yogurt.
So I created this granola...it is so yummy!

2 c. rolled oats, uncooked
1/2 c. raw walnuts or other nuts,
   chopped
1 t. orange zest

1 t. sea salt
1/3 c. sugar-free maple syrup
1/4 c. canola oil

In a bowl, combine oats, nuts, orange zest and salt; mix well. Combine syrup and oil in a separate bowl. Pour over oat mixture; mix well. Spoon mixture onto a parchment paper-lined baking sheet. Bake at 325 degrees for 30 minutes, stirring every 10 minutes. Remove from oven; allow to cool. Store in an airtight container. Makes 8 servings.

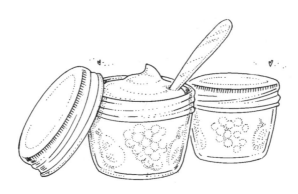

Half-pint Mason jars are just right for filling with layers of fresh fruit, creamy yogurt and crunchy granola. They can even be popped into the fridge the night before, then topped with cereal just before serving. Add a spoon and breakfast is served!

Peach Pie Smoothie

*Lisa Ann DiNunzio
Vineland, NJ*

Refreshing and oh-so good!

1/4 c. almond milk or regular
   milk
1 c. non-fat plain Greek yogurt
1 c. frozen unsweetened peaches
1 to 2 T. honey or pure maple
   syrup

1/2 t. vanilla extract
1/4 t. cinnamon
1/8 t. nutmeg
1 c. ice cubes

Combine all ingredients into a blender and blend until smooth. Serve
in tall glasses. Makes 2 servings.

Perfect Purple Smoothie

*Elizabeth McCord
Bartlett, TN*

*Smoothies are one of my favorite treats and I love creating
new variations. This one is a favorite!*

1-1/2 c. frozen mixed fruit
1-1/4 c. frozen blueberries
1 to 1-1/2 c. orange juice
1/2 c. milk

1/4 c. rolled oats, uncooked
1/2 c. vanilla Greek yogurt or
   regular yogurt
6 ice cubes

Combine all ingredients into a blender. Blend very well until oats are
thoroughly mixed in. Serve in tall glasses. Makes 2 servings.

Hang an old-fashioned peg rack
inside the back door...you'll
always know where to find your
car keys, the kids' backpacks
and the dog's leash!

Krista's Breakfast Tacos

Krista Marshall
Fort Wayne, IN

*I created these fun and tasty tacos for breakfast or brunch
when I discovered taco-size tortillas are easier for my son Alex
to handle than the large burrito-size ones.*

1 lb. mild or hot ground pork
   breakfast sausage
1 green pepper, finely chopped
3 to 4 tomatoes, chopped and
   divided
8 eggs, beaten

2 T. whipping cream
1 c. shredded taco-blend cheese,
   divided
salt and pepper to taste
8 taco-size flour tortillas

In a large skillet over medium heat, brown sausage until no longer
pink. Drain sausage and remove to a bowl, reserving one tablespoon
drippings; set aside. In same skillet, sauté green pepper and half of
tomatoes in reserved drippings until tender. In a large bowl, whisk
eggs, cream, 1/3 cup cheese, salt and pepper. When pepper mixture is
tender, reduce heat to low; add egg mixture and sausage. Cook over
low heat, stirring constantly, until eggs are scrambled and cooked
through, about 10 minutes. Fill tortillas with egg mixture. Top with
remaining tomatoes and cheese. Makes 8 tacos.

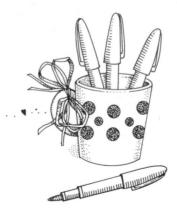

Use a permanent-ink pen on a dry-erase message board to list
kitchen staples like milk, bread, cheese and eggs. Post the board
on the fridge and check off items with a dry-erase pen as they
are used up. On shopping day, just copy the list...simple!

Bacon-Cheddar Biscuits

Suzanne Ramey
Allendale, MI

*A fast and easy Saturday breakfast. Make it even speedier with
1/2 cup of real bacon bits...no skillet to wash!*

2 slices bacon, diced
2 c. biscuit baking mix
2/3 c. milk

1/2 c. shredded Cheddar cheese
1 T. fresh chives, chopped
2 T. butter, melted

In a skillet over medium heat, cook bacon until crisp. Remove bacon to paper towels to drain. In a bowl, combine biscuit mix, milk, cheese and chives. Crumble bacon and add to mixture; stir just until a soft dough forms. Drop dough onto an ungreased baking sheet by heaping tablespoonfuls. Bake at 450 degrees for 8 to 10 minutes, until golden. Brush biscuits with melted butter; serve warm. Makes 8 biscuits.

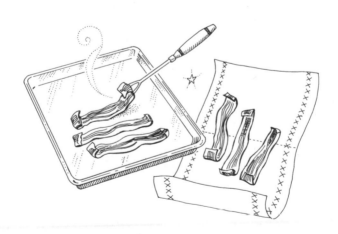

Enjoy all the scrumptious flavor of bacon with none of the mess! Arrange bacon slices on a baking sheet. Bake at 350 degrees for 15 to 20 minutes, until it's as crisp as you like. Drain well on paper towels.

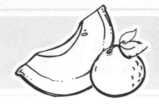

Peanut Butter Apple–Bacon Sandwich

Irene Whatling
West Des Moines, IA

My family loves this grilled sandwich. I even make it for snacks, not just breakfast! It's very satisfying on a cool morning. Sometimes I add some mild Cheddar cheese instead of the peanut butter.

8 slices applewood smoked
   bacon
8 slices whole-grain bread
1/4 c. peach preserves
1 to 2 apples, cored and thinly
   sliced

1/4 c. creamy peanut butter
2 to 3 T. butter, softened and
   divided

In a skillet over medium heat, cook bacon until crisp; drain bacon on paper towels. Spread 4 slices of bread with preserves; layer apple and bacon slices over preserves. Spread remaining bread slices with peanut butter; close sandwiches. Spread tops of sandwiches with half of butter. Place sandwiches butter-side down on a griddle over medium heat. Spread remaining butter on unbuttered side of sandwiches. Cook 2 to 3 minutes per side, until bread is toasted and sandwiches are heated through. Serve warm. Makes 4 sandwiches.

Make some yogurt pops for kids on the go. Insert wooden treat sticks through the tops of a pack of individual yogurts and freeze overnight.

Find Gooseberry Patch
wherever you are!

www.gooseberrypatch.com

Call us toll-free at 1·800·854·6673

U.S. to Metric Recipe Equivalents

Volume Measurements

1/4 teaspoon	1 mL
1/2 teaspoon	2 mL
1 teaspoon	5 mL
1 tablespoon = 3 teaspoons	15 mL
2 tablespoons = 1 fluid ounce	30 mL
1/4 cup	60 mL
1/3 cup	75 mL
1/2 cup = 4 fluid ounces	125 mL
1 cup = 8 fluid ounces	250 mL
2 cups = 1 pint =16 fluid ounces	500 mL
4 cups = 1 quart	1 L

Weights

1 ounce	30 g
4 ounces	120 g
8 ounces	225 g
16 ounces = 1 pound	450 g

Oven Temperatures

300° F	150° C
325° F	160° C
350° F	180° C
375° F	190° C
400° F	200° C
450° F	230° C

Baking Pan Sizes

Square

8x8x2 inches	2 L = 20x20x5 cm
9x9x2 inches	2.5 L = 23x23x5 cm

Rectangular

13x9x2 inches	3.5 L = 33x23x5 cm

Loaf

9x5x3 inches	2 L = 23x13x7 cm

Round

8x1-1/2 inches	1.2 L = 20x4 cm
9x1-1/2 inches	1.5 L = 23x4 cm

Peanut Butter & Jelly French Toast
Judy Lange
Imperial, PA

Every kid loves peanut butter and jelly. What a special morning treat this is...yum!

12 slices favorite bread
3/4 c. creamy peanut butter
6 T. favorite jelly or jam
3 eggs, beaten
3/4 c. milk
1/4 t. salt
2 T. butter, sliced

Spread 6 slices of bread with peanut butter. Spread jelly or jam on remaining slices; combine to form sandwiches. In a shallow bowl, whisk together eggs, milk and salt. Dip sandwiches into egg mixture, coating well on both sides. Melt butter in a skillet over medium heat. Place sandwiches in skillet and cook until golden on both sides. Serve warm. Makes 6 sandwiches.

Breakfast Milkshake
Gladys Kielar
Whitehouse, OH

Children love this fruit-filled shake.

2 ripe bananas, sliced into
   1-inch chunks
1/4 c. blueberries
5 to 10 whole strawberries,
   quartered and hulled
1/2 c. milk

Combine fruits in a plastic freezer bag; seal and freeze for 3 hours to overnight. Place the frozen fruits in a blender or food processor. If fruits are rock-hard, let them thaw a little. Add milk and process until smooth and thick. Pour into mugs and serve with spoons. Makes 2 servings.

Bananas will ripen quickly if placed overnight in a brown paper grocery bag.

Hannah's Bran Mash Muffins

Hannah Klumb
Wisconsin Rapids, WI

*On rainy days, I like to bake these muffins as a
pick-me-up. They make a delicious and healthy breakfast
that starts the day off right.*

1-1/2 c. bran flake cereal
1 c. all-purpose flour
3/4 c. raisins
1/4 c. brown sugar, packed
1 t. baking powder
1/2 t. salt

1 egg, beaten
1 c. milk
1/4 c. oil
1/2 c. carrot, peeled and finely
   shredded
1/2 c. shredded coconut

In a large bowl, combine cereal, flour, raisins, brown sugar, baking powder and salt; mix well. In a separate bowl, whisk together egg, milk and oil. Add egg mixture to cereal mixture; stir in carrot and coconut. Mix everything until just moistened. Pour batter into paper-lined muffin cups, filling nearly full as muffins will not rise much. Bake at 400 degrees for 20 to 22 minutes, until tops are golden. Makes 15 muffins.

For the tenderest muffins and quick breads, stir batter
just until moistened...a few lumps won't matter!

Cinnamon–Pecan Sticky Buns

Crystal Shook
Catawba, NC

A warm, sweet home-baked treat that's ready in a jiffy.

1/3 c. butter, sliced
1/2 c. brown sugar, packed
1/2 c. chopped pecans

1 t. cinnamon
16-oz. tube refrigerated
   biscuits

Melt butter in a 9" round cake pan in the oven at 350 degrees; tilt to coat pan. Mix brown sugar, pecans and cinnamon in a small bowl; sprinkle over melted butter. Arrange biscuits in pan with sides touching (biscuits will fit tightly). Bake at 350 degrees for 25 to 30 minutes, until biscuits are golden and centers of biscuits are fully baked. Invert pan immediately onto a serving plate. Spread any remaining topping from pan on top of buns. Serve warm. Makes 8 buns.

When strawberries are in season, make freezer preserves to enjoy at breakfast...it's easy! Combine one pound ripe strawberries, 1-1/2 cups sugar and 2 tablespoons lemon juice. Bring to a boil, lower heat and simmer, uncovered, for 30 minutes. Spoon into sterilized freezer containers; keep frozen for up to 6 months.

Raisin French Toast Bake

Jill Ball
Highland, UT

This is a weekend favorite with my family...it's easy and yummy.

5 c. cinnamon raisin bread,
    cubed
4 eggs, beaten
1-1/2 c. milk

1/4 c. sugar
1 t. vanilla extract
3 T. butter, cubed and softened
2 t. cinnamon

Place bread cubes in a lightly buttered 8"x8" baking pan. In a bowl, beat together eggs, milk, sugar and vanilla until mixed. Pour mixture over bread cubes. Dot with butter. Let stand about 10 minutes, until bread has absorbed liquid. Sprinkle with cinnamon. Bake at 350 degrees until golden on top, 45 to 50 minutes. Serve warm. Makes 6 servings.

Tempt fussy kids with grilled cheese sandwiches for breakfast. Grilled peanut butter sammies are tasty too. Toast the sandwiches on a waffle iron instead of a griddle...kids will love 'em!

Soup *of the* Day
& Fresh Bread *Too*

Beef Barley Soup

Laura Fredlund
Papillion, NE

*My grandmother is an amazing cook. I have her to thank for my love
of food and cooking for those I love. When I was a little girl, her Beef
Barley Soup became my favorite. Every time I eat this soup I am filled
with wonderful memories...it is scrumptious!*

1-1/2 lbs. ground beef
1 onion, chopped
3 stalks celery, sliced
28-oz. can diced tomatoes
3 10-1/2 oz. cans beef
    consommé

10-3/4 oz. can tomato soup
4 carrots, peeled and chopped
2 c. water
1/2 c. pearled barley, uncooked
1 bay leaf

In a large soup pot over medium heat, cook beef, onion and celery until
beef is no longer pink; drain. Stir in tomatoes with juice and remaining
ingredients; bring to a boil. Reduce heat to low. Simmer, uncovered, for
one hour to 90 minutes, until barley is tender. Stir occasionally.
Discard bay leaf at serving time. Makes 10 to 12 servings.

A flexible plastic cutting mat makes speedy work of
slicing and dicing. Keep two mats on hand for
chopping veggies and meat separately.

Brayden's Feel–Better Vegetable Soup

Shonnie Sims
Canton, GA

*My oldest son loves this soup. Whenever he is under the weather
or just wants something warm, he asks for his special soup...
he thinks it's magic!*

1 lb. ground beef
2 32-oz. containers beef broth
1 cube beef bouillon
14-1/2 oz. can diced tomatoes

1 to 2 12-oz. pkgs. frozen
   mixed soup vegetables
1 to 2 c. elbow macaroni,
   uncooked

Brown beef in a soup pot over medium heat; drain. Add beef broth,
bouillon cube, tomatoes with juice and frozen vegetables. Bring to a
boil; reduce heat to medium-low and cook until vegetables are tender.
Stir in macaroni. Simmer until macaroni is tender, 10 to 15 minutes.
Makes 6 to 8 servings.

Quick Biscuits

Vicki Meredith
Grandview, IN

*I use this simple recipe on busy days and they are quick & easy
to make. They have a hint of sweetness to them. They go fast...
you might want to double the recipe!*

1 c. self-rising flour
1 T. sugar

1 T. mayonnaise
1/2 c. milk

Combine all ingredients in a bowl; mix well. Fill 6 greased muffin cups
1/2 full. Bake at 400 degrees for 12 minutes, or until golden on top.
Serve warm. Makes 6 biscuits.

To equal one cup self-rising flour, substitute
one cup all-purpose flour plus 1-1/2 teaspoons baking
powder and 1/2 teaspoon salt.

Brandy's Broccoli-Cheese Soup
Gabriel Waller
Royal, AR

I first tasted this soup at a friend's house...her mom cooked it for us and it was so good I had to get the recipe!

2 boneless, skinless chicken
   breasts
7 to 8 c. water
6 cubes chicken bouillon
1 bunch broccoli, chopped
3/4 c. cabbage, chopped

3/4 c. carrots, peeled and
   chopped
1-1/4 c. whipping cream
5 slices American cheese
salt and pepper to taste

In a large saucepan, cover chicken with water; add bouillon cubes. Bring to a boil over medium-high heat. Reduce heat to low; simmer until chicken is tender, about 20 minutes. Remove chicken to a bowl, reserving 6 cups broth in saucepan. Add vegetables and cook until tender, 15 to 20 minutes. Cut chicken into bite-size pieces and add to pan along with cream, cheese, salt and pepper. Stir until warmed through and cheese is melted. Makes 4 to 6 servings.

Make your own flavorful chicken broth. Freeze roast chicken bones and when you have two to three carcasses saved, place them in a large slow cooker. Add some chopped carrots, celery and onion; cover with water. Cover and cook on low setting for eight to ten hours. Strain broth and pour into recipe-size containers; refrigerate or freeze.

Cauliflower Soup

Ann Mathis
Biscoe, AR

This delicious soup will really warm you up on a chilly day.

1 head cauliflower, broken
    into flowerets
1 to 2 carrots, peeled and
    shredded
1-1/2 c. celery, chopped
2-1/2 c. water
2 cubes chicken bouillon

3 T. butter, sliced
3 T. all-purpose flour
3/4 t. salt
1/8 t. pepper
2 c. milk
1 c. shredded Cheddar cheese
Optional: 1/2 t. hot pepper sauce

In a large soup pot over medium heat, combine vegetables, water and bouillon cubes. Bring to a boil. Reduce heat to low; cover and simmer for 12 to 15 minutes, until vegetables are tender. Do not drain. Meanwhile, in a large saucepan, melt butter over low heat. Stir in flour, salt and pepper until smooth. Gradually stir in milk; bring to a boil over medium heat. Cook and stir for 2 minutes, or until thickened. Reduce heat to low; stir in cheese until melted. Add hot sauce, if desired. Add cheese mixture to vegetable mixture; gently heat through. Makes 8 servings.

To create a thick, creamy vegetable or bean soup without adding any cream, use a hand–held immersion blender to purée some of the cooked veggies right in the saucepan.

41

Italian Sausage Soup

Goreta Brown
Alberta, Canada

*This soup is scrumptious and full of flavor. Serve it as
a main meal or as a starter to a dinner.*

1 lb. spicy or mild Italian pork
    sausage, sliced or diced
1 to 2 onions, chopped
2 russet potatoes, peeled, halved
    lengthwise and thinly sliced
2 cloves garlic, minced
2 c. chicken broth

4 c. water
2 c. fresh kale or Swiss chard,
    chopped
salt and pepper to taste
1 c. whipping cream or
    half-and-half

Brown sausage in a soup pot over medium heat. Remove sausage with
a slotted spoon and set aside, reserving drippings in pot. Add onions to
pot and cook until softened. Add potatoes and garlic; cook and stir for
one minute. Add chicken broth and water. Cook over medium heat for
15 minutes, stirring occasionally. Stir in sausage, kale or chard, salt
and pepper. Simmer for another 15 minutes, or until potatoes are
tender. Reduce heat to low; stir in cream or half-and-half. Cook and
stir for one minute, until warmed through. Makes 4 servings.

Get together with friends, neighbors and family for a soup
supper...how cozy! Invite everyone to bring their favorite
veggies and cook up a big pot of hearty vegetable soup
together. While the soup simmers, catch up on
conversation or play board games together.

Cheesy Onion Rolls

Amy Hunt
Traphill, NC

These rolls are great for any special supper you're serving.

1/2 c. butter, melted
1 c. grated Parmesan cheese

1.35-oz. pkg. onion soup mix
20 frozen dinner rolls

Spray a 13"x9" baking pan with non-stick vegetable spray; set aside. Place melted butter in a small bowl. Combine Parmesan cheese and soup mix in a medium bowl. Coat each roll thoroughly with butter; roll in cheese mixture. Arrange rolls in baking pan. Cover with a piece of plastic wrap sprayed with non-stick spray. Let rise in a warm place until double in size, about 45 to 60 minutes. Remove plastic wrap. Bake at 350 degrees for 30 to 35 minutes, until golden. Serve warm. Makes 20 rolls.

Italian Dinner Rolls

Susan Wilson
Johnson City, TN

These rolls are very tasty...can't believe they are not made from scratch. So easy to prepare.

10-oz. tube refrigerated flaky
   buttermilk biscuits
1/4 c. butter, melted

1/4 t. garlic powder
1/2 c. grated Parmesan cheese

Separate biscuits; set aside. In a bowl, mix melted butter with garlic powder. Dip each biscuit in butter mixture; shape into a crescent shape. Place biscuits on an ungreased baking sheet. Top biscuits generously with Parmesan cheese. Bake at 400 degrees for 8 to 10 minutes, until golden. Serve warm. Makes 10 biscuits.

Vintage tea towels are perfect for lining bread baskets. They'll keep freshly baked rolls toasty warm and add a dash of color to the table.

Spicy Pork & Sweet Potato Chili

Janet Sharp
Milford, OH

This recipe is a wonderful way to use leftover roast pork from dinner. It is a very hearty chili and is good served with cornbread and coleslaw.

1 T. oil
1 onion, chopped
1 sweet potato, peeled and
    cut into 1/2-inch cubes
3 cloves garlic, chopped
15-1/2 oz. can diced tomatoes
4 c. chicken broth

15-1/2 oz. can white beans,
    drained
12-oz. jar tomatillo green salsa
2 T. chili powder
1 bay leaf
1 lb. cooked pork roast, cut into
    1/2-inch cubes

Heat oil in a Dutch oven over medium heat. Add onion, sweet potato and garlic; sauté about 7 minutes. Stir in tomatoes with juice and remaining ingredients except pork cubes. Reduce heat to medium-low and simmer for about 30 minutes, stirring occasionally. Stir in pork cubes; simmer for 5 minutes. Discard bay leaf before serving. Makes 6 to 8 servings.

Do you have a big pot of leftover soup? Be sure to transfer the extra soup into smaller containers before refrigerating or freezing. The soup will reach a safe temperature much more quickly.

Healthier Cornbread

Nikki Booth
Kinderhook, IL

Delicious with your favorite soup, chili or stew.

3/4 c. whole-wheat flour
1/4 c. all-purpose flour
1 c. cornmeal
1 T. baking powder
Optional: 1 T. ground flax seed

1 egg, beaten
1-1/4 c. 2% milk
1/4 c. canola oil
Garnish: honey

Line an 8"x8" glass baking pan with aluminum foil; spray with non-stick vegetable spray and set aside. Combine all ingredients except garnish in a bowl; mix well. Pour batter into baking pan. Bake at 350 degrees for 20 to 30 minutes. Cut into squares; serve warm with honey. Makes 9 to 12 servings.

Whip up a crock of Honey Bee Butter to serve with warm cornbread. Simply combine one cup honey with one cup softened butter and one teaspoon vanilla extract.

Faster-Than-Stuffed-Cabbage Soup

Tiffani Schulte
Wyandotte, MI

*This is a really hearty soup that couldn't be any simpler to make.
Sometimes I toss a pot together after the dinner dishes are done
so my husband can take it to work the next day for lunch.*

1 onion, diced
1 T. butter
1 T. oil
16-oz. pkg. shredded coleslaw
   mix
16-oz. link Kielbasa pork
   sausage, cut into bite-size
   pieces

28-oz. can crushed tomatoes
2 14-oz. cans beef broth
1-1/2 c. water
1/4 c. brown sugar, packed
1 T. lemon juice
1 t. salt
1 c. long-cooking rice, uncooked
salt and pepper to taste

In a large soup pot, sauté onion in butter and oil until soft, about
5 minutes. Add coleslaw mix and cook for 4 to 5 minutes. Add
Kielbasa and continue cooking several minutes longer. Add tomatoes
with juice, beef broth, water, brown sugar, lemon juice and salt. Bring
to a boil. Stir in rice; return to a boil. Reduce heat to medium-low,
cover and simmer until rice is tender, about 40 minutes. Stir
occasionally. Season with salt and pepper. Makes 6 to 8 servings.

Cloth napkins make mealtime just a little more special...
and they're a must when serving soup! Stitch or hot-glue
fun charms to napkin rings, so family members can
identify their own napkin easily.

Stuffed Pepper Soup

Charlotte Smith
Alexandria, PA

This is a great soup for a chilly day! It's so comforting and delicious. A good way to use some leftover cooked rice too.

1 lb. ground beef
1/2 c. onion, diced
28-oz. can diced tomatoes
1 green pepper, diced

14-oz. can beef broth
2 c. cooked rice
salt and pepper to taste

In a stockpot over medium heat, brown beef with onion; drain. Add tomatoes with juice and remaining ingredients. Reduce heat to medium-low. Simmer until green pepper is tender, about 30 minutes. Makes 6 servings.

Fresh peppers freeze well, so stock up when you find a good sale price. Slice or dice peppers and spread on a baking sheet in a single layer. Freeze for one hour. Transfer peppers to plastic freezer bags, label to be used within 12 months and return to the freezer.

Simple Veggie Soup

Elizabeth McCord
Bartlett, TN

Soups are one of my favorite meals in cool weather. This meatless recipe is a crowd-pleaser. It's colorful, healthy, easy to assemble, it smells wonderful and the flavor is fabulous!

2 14-oz. cans diced tomatoes
15-oz. can kidney beans
15-oz. can green beans, drained
15-oz. can corn, drained
14-1/2 oz. can diced potatoes, drained
4-oz. can sliced mushrooms, drained
1 c. frozen peas

1/2 c. frozen butter beans
1/2 c. frozen lima beans
3 carrots, peeled and diced
1 onion, diced
1/2 c. celery, diced
1 t. Italian seasoning
1 bay leaf
salt and pepper to taste

In a large stockpot, combine tomatoes with juice, kidney beans with liquid and remaining ingredients. Add enough water to completely cover vegetables. Bring to a boil over medium heat. Reduce heat to low and simmer, covered, at least one hour. Stir occasionally. Discard bay leaf before serving. This soup freezes well. Makes 12 servings.

Canned and frozen vegetables are flash-packed soon after being harvested, and they're convenient to keep on hand. If you have fresh-picked veggies available, by all means use them. Generally speaking, a 16-ounce can (drained) or a 16-ounce frozen package equals about 2 cups vegetables.

Apple Cinnamon Bread

Lori Simmons
Princeville, IL

This quick bread is very good. It can be made sugar-free by using low-calorie powdered sweetener, both the regular and the brown sugar kind. Cover the batter completely with apples for a taste of apple in every bite.

1/2 c. brown sugar, packed
1-1/2 t. cinnamon
1/2 c. butter, softened
2/3 c. sugar
2 eggs, beaten
2 t. vanilla extract

1-1/2 c. all-purpose flour
1-1/2 t. baking powder
1/2 c. milk
2 to 3 apples, peeled, cored,
    diced and divided

Mix brown sugar and cinnamon in a cup; set aside. In a large bowl, blend butter and sugar until smooth. Beat in eggs and vanilla. Add flour, baking powder and milk; stir until well moistened. Pour half of batter into a greased 9"x5" loaf pan. Cover with half of chopped apples. Pat apples into batter with back of spoon. Sprinkle with half of brown sugar mixture. Pour remaining batter over apple layer. Top with remaining apples and brown sugar mixture. Pat top of batter with the back of spoon. Bake at 350 degrees for 50 minutes. Let loaf cool in pan for a few minutes on a wire rack; turn loaf out of pan. Makes one loaf.

A new way to enjoy quick bread! Cut into thick slices and butter both sides. Grill or broil until golden and toasted. Sprinkle with powdered sugar and serve with jam.

49

Savory Parmesan Spinach Soup

Myrtle Miller
Providence, KY

Entirely my own creation, this delightful soup uses ingredients you may already have on hand. While budget-friendly and easy to prepare, it really looks like something you would expect to find in a fine dining room. And it tastes as good as it looks!

13-1/2 oz. can chopped spinach, drained
1-1/2 c. water, divided
3/4 c. evaporated milk
1/4 c. grated Parmesan cheese
3 cubes chicken bouillon
1 to 2 cloves garlic, pressed
1 t. butter
1/2 t. dried sage or thyme
1/8 to 1/4 t. pepper
1 bay leaf
Optional: 1/4 t. dried savory, 3 to 4 drops green food coloring
3 T. all-purpose flour
Garnish: additional grated Parmesan cheese

In a large soup pot, combine spinach, 1-1/4 cups water, milk, Parmesan cheese, bouillon cubes, garlic, butter and seasonings. Add optional ingredients, if using. Cook for 10 minutes over medium heat, stirring occasionally. In a bowl, mix flour and remaining water until smooth. Add 1/2 cup of hot spinach mixture to flour mixture. Mix well and stir into soup pot. Cook, stirring often, until thickened. Discard bay leaf. Serve soup topped with Homemade Croutons and a sprinkle of Parmesan cheese. Makes 3 to 4 servings.

Homemade Croutons:

1 to 2 T. butter, softened
1 clove garlic, pressed
1/2 t. dried oregano
4 to 5 slices French bread
grated Parmesan cheese to taste

Blend butter, garlic and oregano; spread on bread. Sprinkle with Parmesan cheese. Place bread on an ungreased baking sheet. Bake at 350 degrees until dry and lightly golden, 10 to 15 minutes. Cool and cube.

Curly Kale Soup

Bev Fisher
Mesa, AZ

I love coming up with new soup recipes! It is fun to share with my neighbors. I love to see them enjoy the foods I take to them. If you have homemade broth to use in this recipe, so much the better.

8 c. chicken broth
1-1/2 lbs. fresh kale, ribs
    discarded and leaves finely
    chopped
1/2 c. onion, minced

4 eggs, beaten
1/4 c. lemon juice
Garnish: shredded Parmesan
    cheese

Bring broth to a boil in a heavy saucepan over medium heat. Add kale and onion. Reduce heat to medium-low and simmer until kale is tender, about 20 minutes. Remove pan from heat; allow mixture to cool to room temperature. Once cooled, whisk together eggs and lemon juice in a bowl; whisk into soup. Warm soup over very low heat; do not boil. Ladle soup into bowls. Serve with Parmesan cheese on the side. Makes 4 servings.

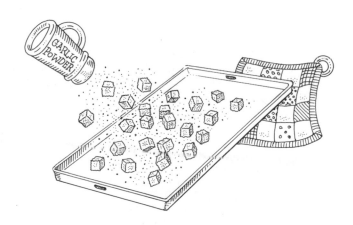

Homemade croutons add a special touch to soup and salad. Cube day-old bread, toss with olive oil and sprinkle with your favorite seasonings. Spread on a baking sheet and bake at 350 degrees for just a few minutes, until crisp.

Colorful Chicken & Squash Soup

Jill Jones
Richmond, TX

*I started making this soup when my husband gave up carbs
to lose weight. It is a great soup to warm you up and it's pretty!*

1/2 c. butter, sliced
1/2 lb. mushrooms, chopped
1 red onion, chopped
2 10-3/4 oz. cans cream of
   chicken soup
10 c. water
1 butternut squash, peeled and
   cubed

1 bunch fresh kale, chopped
4 carrots, peeled and chopped
2 zucchini, chopped
4 cooked chicken breasts, cubed
2 cubes chicken bouillon
2 t. salt
2 t. pepper

Melt butter in a large soup pot over medium heat. Add mushrooms and
onion; cook until softened. Add soup and water to pot; whisk well. Stir
in remaining ingredients; bring to a boil over medium-high heat.
Reduce heat to medium-low. Simmer until vegetables are tender,
stirring occasionally, about 30 minutes. Makes 12 to 15 servings.

Busy day ahead? Use your slow cooker to make soup...
it practically cooks itself! Soup can usually be cooked on
the low setting for six to eight hours, or even longer.

Shelia's Awesome Chicken Noodle Soup

Becky Holsinger
Belpre, OH

I got this recipe from a co-worker after she had brought this in for a luncheon we had. I loved it! When I took it to a church dinner, there weren't any leftovers to bring home. It really is the best chicken noodle soup I've ever had!

1-1/2 t. Italian seasoning
1-1/2 t. dried basil
1 t. garlic salt
1 t. salt
1 t. pepper
3 to 4 boneless, skinless chicken
    breasts, cubed
3/4 c. butter, divided

4 stalks celery, finely chopped
1/2 onion, finely chopped
1 c. baby carrots, finely chopped
48-oz. container chicken broth
12-oz. pkg. frozen egg noodles,
    uncooked
32-oz. container chicken broth,
    divided

Combine seasonings in a shallow bowl. Coat chicken cubes with seasonings; set aside. Melt 1/4 cup butter in a skillet. Add chicken and cook until golden, stirring often. Transfer cooked chicken with pan drippings to a stockpot; add vegetables and large container of broth. Simmer over medium heat until vegetables are tender, about 15 minutes. Stir in frozen noodles and remaining butter. Simmer for 30 to 40 minutes, until noodles are cooked. As broth is absorbed by noodles, add remaining broth as needed. Makes 8 servings.

A simple trick to skim the fat from a pot of soup! When you start your soup, place a metal spoon in the freezer. When soup is done, use the chilled spoon to skim the surface. The fat will stick to the spoon.

Spicy Tomato–Dill Soup

Penny Arnold
Louisville, IL

Door County, Wisconsin is one of our family's all-time favorite vacation spots. We found a charming cafe there that had a wonderful tomato soup on the menu. As soon as we got home, I tried to recreate it. Now I make this soup every fall. Serve with fresh French bread... delicious!

1 onion, diced
3 T. olive oil
2 cloves garlic, minced
1 t. sea salt
1/2 t. pepper
28-oz. can crushed tomatoes
2 T. sugar
4 t. dill weed

1 t. Italian seasoning
1/2 t. red pepper flakes, or more
   to taste
46-oz. can tomato juice
1 c. water
Optional: sour cream, olive oil,
   croutons

Sauté onion in olive oil in a stockpot over medium-low heat. Add garlic, salt and pepper; sauté for one to 2 minutes. Add tomatoes with juice, sugar and seasonings; simmer for several more minutes. Stir in tomato juice and water. Bring to a boil. Reduce heat to low and simmer for about 30 minutes. Garnish individual bowls as desired. Makes 8 servings.

Dried herbs and spices add lots of flavor. Save money by buying them in the bulk food aisle and at ethnic groceries, where they can be quite a bargain.

Multi-Grain Spoon Rolls

Lisa Hains
Ontario, Canada

Mmm! Hot from the oven, these convenient rolls will be a favorite at your house too. It's so helpful to be able to make the dough ahead of time, when entertaining, or to only use the amount needed and keep the remaining dough for another meal.

2 c. warm water
1 env. active dry yeast
1 egg, beaten
1/2 c. butter, melted and
   slightly cooled
1/4 c. honey or molasses

1-1/2 c. all-purpose flour
1-1/4 c. rolled oats, uncooked
1 c. whole-wheat flour
1/2 c. yellow cornmeal
2 T. baking powder
1-1/2 t. salt

Heat water until very warm, about 110 to 115 degrees. In a large bowl, dissolve yeast in warm water; let stand for 5 minutes. Stir in egg, butter and honey or molasses. Add remaining ingredients and mix well. Cover and refrigerate overnight. About 30 minutes before dinner, spoon batter into greased muffin cups, filling 2/3 full. Bake at 375 degrees for 25 to 30 minutes, until golden. Batter may be covered and kept refrigerated for up to 4 days before baking. Makes 16 rolls.

Save time when baking...tuck measuring cups into
your countertop canisters. They are ready to scoop
out flour and sugar when you need them.

Grandma's Garage Sale Soup

Tracy Stoll
Seville, OH

*My grandma always made this soup for us while my mom,
my sister and I were having a garage sale. She knew we
would be too busy to stop and make lunch.*

1 lb. ground beef
1 onion, chopped
1 c. celery, chopped
1/2 c. green pepper, chopped
4 carrots, peeled and sliced
1-1/2 c. water

3 to 4 potatoes, peeled and
    cubed
1/2 t. salt
1/4 t. pepper
4 c. milk
1/3 c. all-purpose flour

Brown beef and onion in a soup pot over medium heat; drain. Add
celery, green pepper and carrots; cook for several minutes. Stir in
water, potatoes and seasonings. Simmer until potatoes are tender,
about 15 minutes. Stir in milk and flour. Cook and stir for several
minutes, until slightly thickened. Makes 4 to 6 servings.

Potatoes can be peeled and cubed ahead of time...
just cover them with water before popping into the
refrigerator. They'll stay nice and white.

Coffee Can Bread

Laurie Rupsis
Aiken, SC

When our children were still at home, I baked this bread in a big coffee can. Now that we're empty nesters, I use soup cans and get five loaves. We can enjoy one and freeze the others for later!

1-1/2 c. raisins
2 c. hot water
2 T. butter, sliced
2 t. baking soda
4 c. all-purpose flour
2 c. sugar

2 eggs, beaten
1 t. cinnamon
1 t. vanilla extract
Optional: 1 c. chopped nuts
Garnish: softened cream cheese

Combine raisins, hot water, butter and baking soda in a large bowl. Cover and let stand at room temperature, 8 hours to overnight. Add remaining ingredients except cream cheese; mix well until a very thick batter forms. Grease and flour three, one-pound metal coffee cans, or five, 10-3/4 ounce soup cans. Spoon batter into cans, filling 1/2 full. Bake at 350 degrees, 50 to 60 minutes for coffee cans, or 40 to 45 minutes for soup cans. Serve warm or at room temperature with cream cheese. Makes 3 regular loaves or 5 mini loaves.

Baking together is a fun family activity and a great choice for kids just starting to learn how to cook. As you measure and mix, be sure to share any stories about hand-me-down recipes. You'll be creating memories as well as sweet treats!

Caldo de Pollo

Courtney Stultz
Columbus, KS

On cold winter nights, our family loves this spicy, hearty chicken soup. It features great Mexican flavors for a tasty dish! It is also very customizable...just substitute your favorite meat or seafood for the chicken. If your grocery doesn't have chayote squash, substitute yellow squash or some more zucchini.

2 boneless, skinless chicken breasts, cooked and shredded
3 to 4 c. chicken broth
1 chayote squash, peeled and diced
1/2 head cabbage, finely chopped
1 to 2 carrots, peeled and diced
1 to 2 zucchini, peeled and diced
1 to 2 potatoes, peeled and diced
1/4 c. fresh cilantro, finely chopped
1 jalapeño pepper, finely chopped
juice of 1 lime
1 t. sea salt
1/2 t. pepper
Garnish: additional cilantro, sliced avocado, salsa

In a large stockpot over medium heat, combine all ingredients except garnish. Bring to a boil; reduce heat to low. Cover and simmer for about 40 minutes, until vegetables are tender. Serve garnished as desired. Makes 6 servings.

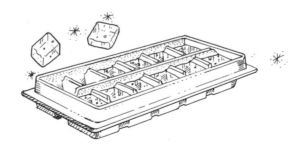

It's easy to save leftover fresh herbs. Spoon chopped herbs into an ice cube tray, one tablespoon per cube. Cover with water and freeze. Frozen cubes can be dropped right into hot stews or soups.

Tex-Mex Salsa Soup

Andrea Heyart
Savannah, TX

If there's any left of this flavorful soup, sometimes I like to give it
a creamy makeover and add a can of Cheddar cheese soup
before reheating. Two different cozy soups from one pot!

1 lb. ground beef	salt and pepper to taste
4 c. beef broth	tortilla chips
24-oz. jar salsa	Garnish: shredded Cheddar
10-oz. can black beans	cheese, sour cream, chopped
3/4 c. dried lentils	fresh cilantro
1 t. ground cumin	

Brown beef in a stockpot over medium heat; drain. Add remaining
ingredients except tortilla chips and garnish. Bring to a boil. Reduce
heat to medium-low. Cover and simmer for 30 to 40 minutes, stirring
occasionally, until lentils are soft. Serve with tortilla chips; garnish as
desired. Makes 8 servings.

Do you have a jar that's really hard to open? Gently insert the tip
of a blunt table knife under the edge of the lid. That's usually
enough to break the vacuum, allowing the lid to twist right off.

Pat's Lentil & Ham Soup

Pat Martin
Riverside, CA

Always the dilemma about the leftover ham bone...what to make, split pea soup or lentil soup? This lentil soup wins my vote, as it is hearty and full of vegetables. The next day it is out-of-this-world good! Hubby hums while he eats it.

2 T. olive oil
1 onion, chopped
2 carrots, peeled and diced
2 c. dried brown lentils
8 c. low-sodium chicken broth
1 t. garlic powder or garlic salt
1/2 t. dried thyme

1/4 t. red pepper flakes
1 bay leaf
1 meaty ham bone
2 russet potatoes, peeled and
  diced
2 c. cooked ham, chopped
salt and pepper to taste

Heat oil in a Dutch oven over medium heat; add onion, carrots and lentils. Cook until vegetables are softened, about 5 minutes. Stir in broth and seasonings; bring to a boil. Add ham bone and potatoes; reduce heat to medium-low. Simmer, covered, until thickened and lentils are tender, about one hour, stirring occasionally. Discard ham bone and bay leaf. Ladle 1/4 to 1/2 of soup into a blender; cover and process carefully until smooth. Return puréed soup to pot. May also use an immersion blender to purée some of soup right in the pot, while leaving it chunky but thick. Stir in ham. Cover and simmer about 5 minutes, until heated through. Season with salt and pepper. Makes 8 servings.

Dried beans are nutritious, inexpensive and come in lots of varieties...perfect for delicious family meals. Before cooking, place beans in a colander, rinse well and pick through, discarding any small twigs or bits of debris.

Beer Yeast Bread

Nanette Hayles
Port Neches, TX

This bread is wonderful! It's super easy, quick to make and makes your home smell incredible. I make it and share with friends. One friend's husband exclaimed, "You make bread, too!" I hope it isn't becoming a lost art.

2-1/2 c. all-purpose flour
2 T. sugar
1 t. caraway seed
1/2 t. salt
1 env. active dry yeast

1 c. beer or non-alcoholic beer
1 T. butter
1 T. honey
1 egg, beaten

In a large bowl, combine flour, sugar, caraway seed, salt and yeast; mix well and set aside. In a small saucepan over low heat, combine beer, butter and honey. Heat to very warm; add to flour mixture along with egg. Stir well; beat with an electric mixer on medium speed for 2 minutes. Cover dough and let rise in a warm place for 30 minutes. Stir down dough; transfer to a greased and floured 9"x5" loaf pan. Cover and let rise for 15 minutes. Uncover and bake at 375 degrees for 30 to 35 minutes, until deeply golden. Remove loaf from pan; cool for several minutes before slicing. Makes one loaf.

Fresh-baked, cooled bread freezes beautifully. Wrap it in plastic, then aluminum foil and freeze for up to three weeks. Add a ribbon bow for a delightful hostess gift.

Corn Chowder

Renee Johnson
Cookeville, TN

This chowder is wonderful on a cool fall night with a crisp salad or a grilled cheese sandwich. It's been a favorite for many years. I often use fat-free half-and-half, and when I do, I usually add a little cornstarch at the end to thicken it a bit.

2 T. butter, divided
1/4 lb. country ham, diced
3 c. onions, diced
1 bay leaf
3/4 c. homestyle white bread,
   torn into crumbs
2 c. chicken broth

2 c. water
3 c. potatoes, peeled and diced
1 red pepper, chopped
1 green pepper
2 c. corn, thawed if frozen
2 c. half-and-half
salt and pepper to taste

In a stockpot over medium heat, melt one tablespoon butter. Add ham and sauté for about 5 minutes. Stir in onions; add bay leaf. Cover and cook for 8 to 10 minutes, until onions are tender. Stir in bread crumbs; add broth, water and potatoes. Bring to a boil; reduce heat to low. Partially cover and simmer for 20 minutes, or until potatoes are tender. Meanwhile, melt remaining butter in a skillet over medium heat. Sauté peppers until tender, about 5 minutes. Add pepper mixture to stockpot along with corn and half-and-half. Simmer for 2 to 3 minutes, until warmed through. Discard bay leaf; season with salt and pepper. Makes 6 to 8 servings.

Get out Grandma's cast-iron skillet for the tastiest, toastiest hot sandwiches. Cast iron provides even heat distribution for speedy cooking and crisp golden crusts.

Cristina's Cheddar Cheese Biscuits

Cristina Davenport
Lehi, UT

After tasting some Cheddar cheese biscuits at a chain restaurant, I decided to create my own version. My husband, who is a very good food critic, says that my biscuits are better than the ones they serve at the restaurant!

2 c. biscuit baking mix
1 c. plus 2 T. coarsely shredded
   sharp Cheddar cheese
2/3 c. milk

3/4 t. garlic powder
1/2 t. dried parsley
1/4 t. onion powder
1/8 t. garlic salt

In a large bowl, combine all ingredients. Mix with a wooden spoon until a soft dough forms; beat vigorously for 30 seconds. Drop dough by heaping tablespoonfuls onto an ungreased baking sheet. Bake at 450 degrees for 8 to 10 minutes, until golden. Brush Butter Topping over hot biscuits before removing from baking sheet. Serve warm. Makes 14 biscuits.

Butter Topping:

1/4 c. butter, melted
1/4 to 1/2 t. garlic powder

1/2 t. dried parsley

Stir together all ingredients in a cup.

For uniform-sized biscuits,
use an ice cream scoop
to portion out dough.

Hearty Italian Chili

Molly Carter
Powersville, MO

*I started making this chili when my husband and I were dating.
With a couple of minor tweaks, it soon became one of his favorites.*

1 lb. ground beef
1/2 lb. ground Italian pork
  sausage
1 onion, chopped
1/2 c. green pepper, chopped
14-1/2 oz. can diced tomatoes
26-oz. jar spaghetti sauce
1 c. water

16-oz. can kidney beans,
  drained and rinsed
14-1/2 oz. can sliced
  mushrooms, drained
1/3 c. pepperoni slices, halved
1 t. chili powder
1/2 t. salt
1/8 t. pepper

In a large saucepan over medium heat, cook beef, sausage, onion and
green pepper until meats are no longer pink; drain. Stir in tomatoes
with juice and remaining ingredients; bring to a boil. Reduce heat to
low. Simmer, uncovered, for 30 minutes, stirring occasionally. Makes
6 to 8 servings.

A hometown chili cook-off! Ask neighbors to bring a pot of
their best "secret recipe" chili to share, then have a friendly
judging for the best. You provide lots of crackers and buttered
cornbread, cool drinks and bright red bandannas for
terrific lap-size napkins.

Tuscan Bean Soup

Mary Rose Kulczak
Noblesville, IN

Serve this savory soup with warm crusty bread for a hearty meal!

1/2 c. red onion, diced
1/2 to 1 c. celery, chopped
2 cloves garlic, minced
2 to 3 T. olive oil
14-1/2 oz. can Italian-style
   diced tomatoes
15-1/2 oz. can Great Northern
   beans, drained and rinsed

3 14-oz. cans chicken broth
1 to 2 t. Italian seasoning
1/4 t. red pepper flakes
salt and pepper to taste
2 c. fresh spinach, chopped
Garnish: shredded Parmesan
   cheese

In a large stockpot over medium heat, sauté onion, celery and garlic in olive oil until tender. Stir in tomatoes with juice, beans, broth and seasonings. Bring to a low boil; reduce heat to low. Simmer, stirring occasionally, for 20 to 30 minutes. Stir in spinach; simmer for 2 to 3 minutes. Ladle into soup bowls and top with Parmesan cheese. Makes 4 to 6 servings.

Need to add a little flavor boost to a pot of soup? Just add a splash of cider vinegar, lemon juice or Worcestershire sauce.

Liz's Pierogie Soup

Liz Lanza
Charles Town, WV

This is a modern take on classic noodle soup. The filling in the pierogies breaks down and creates a thick soup that is a hit with young and old.

15-oz. pkg. frozen potato and
    cheese pierogies
2 T. butter
1/2 c. onion, chopped
1 c. cabbage, finely chopped
    and packed
3-1/2 c. chicken broth

1/4 t. garlic powder
1/4 t. salt
1/4 t. pepper
1/4 t. paprika
1 c. milk
1 c. shredded Cheddar cheese

Partially thaw pierogies for a few minutes. Cut pierogies into bite-sized pieces and set aside. Melt butter in a large saucepan over medium heat. Add onion and cabbage; sauté for 5 to 7 minutes, until onion is translucent. Stir in pierogies, broth and seasonings; bring to a boil. Reduce heat to low and simmer for about 15 minutes, stirring occasionally. Add milk and cheese. Cook and stir over low heat until warmed through and cheese melts, about 5 minutes. Makes 6 servings.

Freshen the garbage disposal while sharpening the blades at the same time. Pour white vinegar into an ice cube tray and freeze. Drop the cubes, one at a time, into the disposal while it's running.

Peppery Greek Yogurt Cheddar Biscuits

Marie Matter
Dallas, TX

*Greek yogurt lends a great tang and fluffy texture
to these savory biscuits.*

1-1/2 c. self-rising flour
1 t. kosher salt
1 t. pepper
1-1/4 c. plain Greek yogurt

3/4 c. shredded white Cheddar
   cheese
1 egg, beaten

Mix together flour, salt and pepper in a bowl. Create a well in the
center; add yogurt and stir until just blended. Add cheese and stir
briefly. Turn dough out onto a lightly floured surface; pat out dough to
about one-inch thick. Cut out biscuits using a floured biscuit cutter.
Combine dough scraps and roll out again to make remaining biscuits.
Place biscuits on a parchment paper-lined baking sheet; brush the tops
with beaten egg. Bake at 450 degrees for 10 to 15 minutes, until
lightly golden on top. Serve warm. Makes 8 biscuits.

Buttery Farm Biscuits

Samantha Reilly
Gig Harbor, WA

*A great biscuit recipe my family has been making for years.
Serve with more butter.*

2 c. all-purpose flour
1 t. baking powder
1/2 t. salt

3/4 c. butter
3/4 c. milk

In a large bowl, mix together flour, baking powder and salt. Cut in
butter with 2 knives until a fine crumble forms. Stir in milk. Flatten
out dough on a well floured surface. Cut into 12 rounds with a biscuit
cutter. Place biscuits close together on an ungreased baking sheet.
Bake at 400 degrees for 15 to 20 minutes, until golden. Serve warm.
Makes one dozen.

Of soup and love, the first is best.
– Spanish Proverb

Bright & Zesty Italian Wedding Soup

Amanda Johnson
Marysville, OH

I developed this special recipe after tasting a similar soup at a local Italian restaurant. I added a special touch of lemon to make it extra bright and tasty. It was an instant family favorite!

49-1/2 oz. can chicken broth
2 t. lemon zest
juice of 1 lemon
1 lb. boneless, skinless chicken
    breasts, cut into bite-size
    pieces

1/2 c. onion, finely diced
1 carrot, peeled and finely diced
8-oz. pkg. acini di pepe pasta,
    uncooked
1/4 c. fresh spinach, finely
    chopped

Add chicken broth, lemon zest and lemon juice to a large stockpot. Bring to a rolling boil over medium-high heat. Add chicken, onion and carrot. Reduce heat to medium-low. Simmer until chicken is cooked through and vegetables are tender, about 30 minutes. Stir in pasta and spinach. Simmer until pasta is tender, an additional 8 to 10 minutes. Makes 6 servings.

Prevent messy pot boil-overs! Rub a little vegetable oil around the top few inches inside the stockpot.

Homestyle Egg Drop Soup

Janis Parr
Ontario, Canada

We enjoy this soup often, even when we aren't having Chinese cuisine. It's simple to make and so delicious!

8 c. chicken broth, divided
1 cube chicken bouillon
3 T. cornstarch

4 eggs, well beaten
2 T. green onion, thinly sliced
salt and pepper to taste

Place 6-1/2 cups broth and bouillon cube in a soup pot over medium-high heat; bring to a boil. In a small bowl, combine cornstarch and remaining 1-1/2 cups broth; stir until dissolved. Pour cornstarch mixture into boiling broth and stir well. With a fork, drizzle eggs into boiling broth; eggs will cook immediately. Add green onion and stir. Add salt and pepper to taste. Reduce heat and simmer for one to 2 minutes. Serve piping hot. Makes 6 servings.

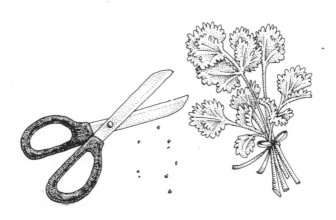

Kitchen shears are so handy! You'll find yourself using them again & again for snipping fresh herbs, chopping tomatoes right in the can and snipping the ends off fresh green beans.

Boston Clam Chowder

Jeannie Hardman
Salt Lake City, UT

This creamy chowder is very satisfying with crusty bread and a crisp salad. Sometimes I use all whole milk instead of the half-and-half and it still turns out great. Don't forget the saltine crackers!

3 c. potatoes, peeled and cubed
1 c. onion, chopped
1 c. celery, chopped
3 6-1/2 oz. cans chopped clams,
    drained and juice reserved
3/4 c. butter

3/4 c. all-purpose flour
1 T. sugar
1 t. salt
1/8 t. pepper
2 c. whole milk
2 c. half-and-half

Place potatoes, onion and celery in a saucepan over medium heat. Add reserved clam juice, setting aside clams. Add enough water to just cover the vegetables. Simmer until tender, about 15 minutes. Do not drain. Meanwhile, melt butter in a heavy large soup pot over medium heat. Add flour, sugar, salt and pepper; blend into a smooth paste. Cook for 5 minutes, stirring often. Add milk and half-and-half; whisk constantly over medium-high heat until smooth and thickened. Stir in potato mixture with cooking liquid. Reduce heat to low; add reserved clams. Simmer for 10 minutes, or until heated through. Makes 8 to 10 servings.

Serve steaming chowder in fresh-baked bread bowls. Scoop out small round loaves of sourdough bread and brush the insides with olive oil. Bake in a 350-degree oven for ten minutes, then fill with hearty soup.

Eat Your Veggies!

Lemony Orzo & Spinach

Lisa Ann DiNunzio
Vineland, NJ

A simple, light side dish that goes well with baked chicken.

16-oz. pkg. orzo pasta,
   uncooked
2 to 3 T. extra virgin olive oil
1 to 2 T. butter, sliced

1/2 t. lemon zest
1 t. lemon juice
1 c. fresh baby spinach
sea salt and pepper to taste

Cook pasta according to package directions; drain and return to saucepan with heat turned off. Add remaining ingredients except salt and pepper; gently toss together. Season with salt and pepper; toss again. Serve warm. Makes 6 servings.

Let the kids lend a hand in the kitchen! Preschoolers can wash veggies, fold napkins and set the table. Older children can measure, shred, chop, stir and maybe even help with meal planning and grocery shopping.

Quick & Easy Cheesy Zucchini

Lori Ritchey
Denver, PA

This simple side dish is delicious with grilled chicken or steak.
Use dried, minced onion to save time, if you like.

1/4 c. onion, finely chopped
2 T. butter, sliced
6 c. zucchini, grated

salt and pepper to taste
1 c. shredded Colby Jack cheese

In a large saucepan over medium-high heat, sauté onion in butter until translucent. Stir in zucchini; season with salt and pepper. Reduce heat to medium. Cook, stirring occasionally, until zucchini is soft and the liquid has evaporated. Add cheese; cook and stir until melted. Serve immediately. Makes 4 servings.

Too many zucchini? Grate extra zucchini and freeze it in two-cup portions...it'll be ready to add to your favorite recipes all winter long.

Spicy Green Beans with Bacon

Kim Jensen
Osceola, WI

These flavor-filled beans are a hit every time!

2 to 3 slices bacon
1/2 onion, diced
1 lb. fresh green beans, trimmed
1/2 t. red pepper flakes

salt and pepper to taste
1/2 c. boiling water
1 T. butter
1-1/2 t. white vinegar

In a large skillet, cook bacon over medium heat until golden. Transfer bacon to a plate with a slotted spoon, reserving drippings in skillet. Add onion to the skillet and cook until softened. Add green beans, red pepper flakes, salt and pepper. Sauté over medium-high heat, stirring, for 2 minutes. Add boiling water and immediately cover the skillet. Steam beans, shaking skillet occasionally, for 15 minutes, or until tender. Add butter, vinegar and additional salt and pepper; toss until combined. Crumble reserved bacon and sprinkle over beans. Serve warm. Makes 6 servings.

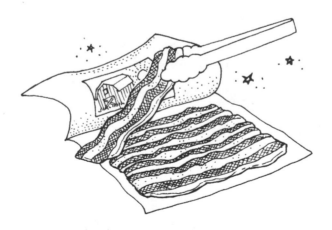

Mmm...is anything better than bacon? To separate bacon slices easily, first let the package stand at room temperature for about 20 minutes.

Cheesy Broccoli Patties

Megan Brooks
Antioch, TN

*Even confirmed broccoli haters are sure to like these crisp,
cheesy patties. Use steamed fresh broccoli if you wish.*

2 t. oil
1/2 onion, chopped
2 cloves garlic, minced
12-oz. pkg. frozen chopped
   broccoli, thawed
3/4 c. panko bread crumbs

1/2 c. shredded sharp Cheddar
   cheese
1/3 c. grated Parmesan cheese
2 eggs, beaten
salt and pepper to taste

Line a baking sheet with aluminum foil; spray with non-stick
vegetable spray and set aside. Heat oil in a small saucepan over
medium heat. Add onion and garlic; cook until tender and remove
from heat. Place broccoli in a large bowl; press out any excess water
with a paper towel. Add onion mixture and remaining ingredients; mix
well and form into 6 to 8 flattened patties. Arrange patties on baking
sheet. Bake, uncovered, at 400 degrees for 15 minutes; carefully turn
patties over. Bake another 15 minutes, until crisp and golden. Serve
warm. Makes 6 to 8 servings.

What was Paradise but a garden, full of vegetables
and herbs and pleasures?

– William Lawson

Roasted Summer Vegetables

Gloria Kaufmann
Orrville, OH

A delicious way to use garden-fresh summer vegetables. Serve as a side dish, or spoon veggies into sandwiches or wraps and top with a dollop of dip.

12 mushrooms, trimmed
1 red pepper, cut into
    1-1/2 inch squares
1 green pepper, cut into
    1-1/2 inch squares
1 red onion, cut into wedges

1 yellow squash, halved and
    cut into 1-1/2 inch pieces
1 T. olive oil
dried thyme, salt and pepper
    to taste

Make Creamy Dip ahead of time; chill. Combine vegetables in a bowl; drizzle with oil and toss to coat. Add seasonings; toss again. Arrange vegetables in a single layer on a lightly greased 15"x10" jelly-roll pan. Bake, uncovered, at 450 degrees for 10 minutes, or until crisp-tender. Serve warm with Creamy Dip. Makes 6 servings.

Creamy Dip:

1/2 c. fat-free mayonnaise
1/4 c. light sour cream

2 T. salsa
1 clove garlic, minced

Combine all ingredients in a bowl. Cover and chill for 30 minutes to overnight.

Need a tiny funnel for filling
salt & pepper shakers? Cut a corner
piece from an envelope, then
snip away the tip.

Eat Your Veggies!

Baked Asparagus

Kelli Venable
Ostrander, OH

*My mom and I tried this recipe on Mothers' Day because it was
too cold outdoors to put it on the grill. It was very good!*

2 bunches asparagus, trimmed
1/4 c. olive oil
2 t. coarse salt

1 t. pepper
1/4 c. grated Parmesan cheese

Place asparagus in a large bowl; drizzle with olive oil and toss gently
to coat. Season with salt and pepper. Arrange asparagus in a single
layer on a lightly greased baking sheet. Sprinkle with Parmesan
cheese. Bake, uncovered, at 375 degrees for 15 to 20 minutes, to
desired doneness. Makes 6 to 8 servings.

Awesome Green Beans

Teresa Eller
Tonganoxie, KS

*I love this recipe! The green beans are tender-crisp with a little
sweetness...they go well with any meat dish I make.*

6 c. water
1 lb. fresh green beans, trimmed
1 onion, chopped

2 to 3 t. oil
1/2 c. soy sauce

In a large saucepan over high heat, bring water to a boil. Add green
beans. Reduce heat to medium-high and cook for about 5 minutes.
Drain; cover beans with ice water and set aside. In a skillet over
medium heat, sauté onion in oil until tender. Add beans and soy sauce
to skillet. Cook over medium heat for 5 to 8 minutes, until beans are
tender and soy sauce is slightly thickened. Makes 4 servings.

Start family meals with a gratitude circle...each person takes a
moment to share something that he or she is thankful for that
day. It's a sure way to put everyone in a cheerful mood!

Beckie's Skillet Trash

Beckie Apple
Grannis, AR

There's nothing my family loves more than fresh vegetables from our own garden! This is a favorite dish that is a combination of our favorites. When our son Michael was young, he would ask, "What all's in here, Mom?" and I'd say "Let's just call it Skillet Trash." And it stuck. He's nearly 40 now and still says, "Mom, what all is in here?" Great served with a pan of hot cornbread.

1/4 c. oil
2 potatoes, peeled and cut in
   1-inch cubes
1 onion, coarsely chopped
2 yellow squash, cut in 1/4-inch
   slices or cubes
1 zucchini, cut in 1/4-inch slices
   or cubes

1 to 2 cucumbers, cut in
   1-inch slices
1/2 lb. mushrooms, thickly
   sliced
1 t. salt
1/2 t. pepper
1/4 t. garlic powder
3 T. soy sauce

Heat oil in a large skillet over medium heat. Add vegetables; sprinkle with seasonings. Sauté over medium heat, stirring often, for 10 to 15 minutes. Reduce heat to medium-low. Continue to cook for 10 minutes, or until vegetables are fork-tender. Remove from heat and add soy sauce. Toss gently and serve. Makes 6 servings.

Enjoy seasonal fruits and veggies...strawberries and asparagus in spring, corn and tomatoes in summer, pears and acorn squash in fall and cabbage and apples in winter. You'll be serving your family the tastiest, healthiest produce year 'round.

Eat Your **Veggies!**

Spinach Pasta Toss

Jan Sherwood
Carpentersville, IL

I used to serve this to my family as a side with chops or chicken.
Now that we are empty nesters, we enjoy it as a main with a fruit
salad and crusty warm bread. It's low-calorie, made in one pan in
15 minutes and tastes terrific...what more could one ask for?

14-1/2 oz. can Italian-style
   diced tomatoes
2 c. multi-grain penne pasta,
   uncooked
1 c. water

9-oz. pkg. fresh baby spinach,
   divided
1 c. shredded Italian 3-cheese
   blend

In a large saucepan, combine tomatoes with juice, uncooked pasta
and water. Bring to a boil over medium-high heat. Reduce heat to
medium-low. Cover and simmer about 10 minutes, just until pasta is
tender. Stir in half of spinach. Cover and cook for 2 minutes, or until
wilted. Repeat with remaining spinach. Serve topped with cheese.
Makes 6 servings.

Italian-Style Polenta

Eleanor Dionne
Beverly, MA

My mom used to make this dish when I was growing up. My uncle
also made it and he added white kidney beans. It is so yummy!
We would serve it on a large platter, covered with tomato sauce.

2 c. milk
2 c. water
1/4 c. butter, sliced

2 c. cornmeal, divided
1/4 c. grated Parmigiano cheese
Optional: warmed tomato sauce

In a large saucepan over medium-low heat, bring milk, water and
butter to a simmer. Be careful not to boil. Slowly whisk in half the
cornmeal until consistency is very thick, but smooth. Whisk in
remaining cornmeal as needed for a thick, smooth consistency. Reduce
heat to low. Simmer for about 30 minutes. Stir in cheese before
serving. Serve with tomato sauce, if desired. Makes 6 servings.

Roasted Winter Vegetables

Gladys Kielar
Whitehouse, OH

*It's almost magical how veggies turn soft and sweet
in the oven...and with so little effort!*

3 c. carrots, peeled and cut into
    1-1/2 inch lengths
3 c. parsnips, peeled and cut into
    1-1/2 inch lengths
2 c. sweet potatoes, peeled and
    cut into 1-1/2 inch cubes

2 c. butternut squash, peeled
    and cut into 1-1/2 inch
    cubes
3 T. olive oil
1 T. fresh thyme, chopped
salt and pepper to taste

Line 2 baking sheets with aluminum foil; oil lightly and set aside.
Combine vegetables in a large bowl. Add olive oil, thyme, salt and
pepper; toss to coat. Divide vegetables between baking sheets,
spreading in a single layer. Bake, uncovered, at 425 degrees for
35 to 40 minutes, stirring twice, until tender and golden. Season with
more salt and pepper, as desired. Makes 10 servings.

Make your own flavorful, nutritious vegetable broth.
In a freezer container, save up carrot peels, celery leaves and
other veggie scraps. When the container is full, place the
veggies in a soup pot, add water to cover and simmer
gently for 30 minutes. Strain before using or freezing.

Eat Your Veggies!

Not Your Granny's Brussels Sprouts

Lynnette Jones
East Flat Rock, NC

Remember those soggy boiled Brussels sprouts Grandma used to serve? No more, with this updated recipe!

2 slices bacon, diced
2 lbs. Brussels sprouts, trimmed
   and halved or quartered
1 T. olive oil
1 t. salt

2 T. pure maple syrup
1 t. cider vinegar
1 t. Chinese 5-spice powder,
   or 1/8 t. cinnamon plus
   1/8 t. pepper

In a skillet over medium heat, cook bacon until crisp. Set bacon aside, reserving one teaspoon drippings. In a large bowl, toss Brussels sprouts with reserved drippings, olive oil and salt. Arrange sprouts on a lightly greased baking sheet. Bake, uncovered, at 350 degrees for 15 to 20 minutes, until just tender. Turn oven to broil. Broil sprouts for 2 to 3 minutes, just until slightly charred. Meanwhile, combine syrup, vinegar and spice in a small saucepan; simmer over low heat for several minutes. Toss sprouts with syrup mixture and reserved bacon. Makes 6 to 8 servings.

A pretty saucer that has lost its teacup makes a useful spoon rest to set by the stovetop.

Uncle Ed's Baked Beans

Sheri Kohl
Wentzville, MO

My brother-in-law Ed was so fond of my baked beans, I made them whenever he came to town. After several visits, my young daughter Brittany began calling them "Uncle Ed's Baked Beans." When I created a family cookbook for her as a wedding present, I included this recipe. We've got Uncle Ed covered, no matter which house he visits!

3 16-oz. cans pork & beans
1/2 c. bacon, crisply cooked
   and crumbled
1/3 c. catsup
3 T. molasses
3 T. honey

2 t. onion, chopped
1-1/2 t. mustard
1 t. smoke-flavored cooking
   sauce
1/2 t. garlic salt
1/4 t. pepper

Combine all ingredients in a lightly greased 1-1/2 quart casserole dish. Stir gently. Bake, uncovered, at 325 degrees for 90 minutes. Makes 10 servings.

A fun and simple meal...try a chili dog bar! Along with steamed hot dogs and buns, set out some hot chili, shredded cheese, sauerkraut, chopped onions and your favorite condiments.

Honey-Mustard Glazed
Sweet Onions

Judy Henfey
Cibolo, TX

Many years ago, I received this recipe through a recipe exchange from a woman in Washington State whom I had never met. I tried the recipe and my family was hooked. It's a great recipe to have on hand when you fire up the grill for chicken or beef.

4 sweet onions, cut into
   8 wedges each
2 T. butter, sliced
1 T. plus 1 t. red wine vinegar
1 T. country-style Dijon mustard

2 t. honey
1/4 t. paprika
1/4 t. salt
pepper to taste

Place onions in a lightly greased casserole dish; set aside. Melt butter in a small saucepan over low heat; stir in remaining ingredients. Pour mixture over onions and stir well to coat. Bake, uncovered, at 350 degrees for 30 minutes or until soft and glazed, stirring occasionally. Serve warm. Makes 6 to 8 servings.

Mix up a zesty Dijon dressing in an almost-empty mustard jar...
delicious on crisp salads, steamed vegetables and broiled fish.
Add 1/2 cup olive oil and 1/3 cup fresh lemon juice to the jar;
shake well. Add salt and pepper to taste. Keep chilled.

Bacon & Onion Foil Packet Potatoes

Susan Griffith
Columbus, OH

You'll love these easy-to-fix potatoes! Perfect for cookouts,
or tuck the packets in the oven alongside ribs or chicken.

10 to 12 new redskin potatoes,
   thinly sliced
12 slices bacon, cooked and
   crumbled
1/2 c. onion, diced
1.35-oz. pkg. onion soup mix

salt and pepper to taste
3 T. butter, sliced
Optional: 1 c. shredded Cheddar
   cheese
Optional: sour cream

Spray 3 long sheets of heavy-duty aluminum foil with non-stick vegetable spray. Top each piece with equal portions of potatoes, bacon and onion. Sprinkle soup mix evenly over top; season with salt and pepper. Add one tablespoon butter to each packet; divide cheese among packets, if using. Seal packets securely. Grill for 20 to 30 minutes, until potatoes are tender. Packets may also be placed on a baking sheet and baked at 350 degrees for about 35 minutes. Let stand 10 minutes before serving. Serve from foil packets, topped with sour cream, if desired. Makes 4 to 6 servings.

Make some tangy pickled veggies next time you finish a jar of dill pickles. Simply cut up fresh carrots, green or red peppers and other vegetables, drop them into the leftover pickle juice and refrigerate for a few days.

Eat Your **Veggies!**

Crispy Golden Parmesan Potatoes

JoAnn

We love potatoes! I'm always tickled to find a tasty new way to fix them. This recipe is scrumptious.

1/4 c. butter, melted and divided
1/2 c. grated Parmesan cheese
1 t. garlic powder

1-3/4 lbs. Yukon gold potatoes, halved lengthwise

Spread one tablespoon melted butter in a 13"x9" baking pan; place remaining butter in a small bowl. Mix cheese and garlic powder in a separate small bowl. Dip cut sides of potatoes into butter, then into cheese mixture. Place cut-side down in baking pan. Drizzle with any remaining butter. Bake, uncovered, at 400 degrees for 30 to 35 minutes, until tender. Makes 6 to 8 servings.

Holly's Potatoes

Paulette Alexander
Newfoundland, Canada

This recipe is named for my niece, who loves potatoes prepared this way. So easy, yet tasty.

4 potatoes, halved lengthwise
1/4 c. butter, melted
1/2 t. onion powder

1/2 t. garlic powder
1/2 t. red pepper flakes
1/2 t. pepper

Brush cut sides of potatoes with half of melted butter; sprinkle with half of seasonings. Turn potatoes over; repeat. Place potatoes cut-side down in a lightly greased 13"x9" baking pan. Bake, uncovered, at 350 degrees for about 30 minutes, until fork-tender. Makes 4 servings.

Tuck an apple into a bag of potatoes to keep the potatoes from sprouting.

Maple–Orange Glazed Carrots

Mel Chencharick
Julian, PA

*This recipe is so simple, yet it gives plain
baby carrots a great new taste.*

3 T. butter, sliced
1/4 c. pure maple syrup
1/4 c. orange juice

1/4 c. water
1/4 t. kosher salt
16-oz. pkg. baby carrots

Melt butter in a saucepan over medium heat. Stir in remaining
ingredients except carrots. Add carrots and toss to coat. Bring to a boil
over medium-high heat, stirring occasionally. Reduce heat to medium-
low. Cover and cook until carrots are tender, about 15 minutes. Serve
carrots with sauce from pan. Makes 6 servings.

A flavorful drizzle for steamed veggies...on the stovetop,
simmer 1/2 cup balsamic vinegar, stirring often,
until thickened. So simple and scrumptious.

Baked Sweet Potatoes with Thyme Butter

Mary Thomason-Smith
Bloomington, IN

Pair these flavorful sweet potatoes with a roast chicken (from the deli, if you like!) and spinach salad for a wonderful meal. Try spreading the delicious butter on hot crusty French bread too.

4 sweet potatoes

Place sweet potatoes on an aluminum foil-lined baking sheet. Pierce potatoes several times with a fork. Bake at 400 degrees for 45 minutes to one hour, until fork-tender. To serve, slice open potatoes. Top each with a slice of Thyme Butter. Makes 4 servings.

Thyme Butter:

1 T. fresh lemon thyme, chopped   1/2 c. butter, softened
2 T. fresh thyme, chopped

In a small bowl, blend chopped herbs into softened butter. Spoon butter mixture onto a piece of plastic wrap. Roll into a log by twisting ends of plastic wrap together; refrigerate.

Fresh herbs will taste their best stored for just a few days in an open or perforated plastic bag in the refrigerator. To keep them up to a week, snip off the ends and arrange them in a tall glass with an inch of water. Cover loosely with a plastic bag and place in the fridge.

Tangy Marinated Beans & Tomatoes

Angie Salayon
New Orleans, LA

My sister Maureen Salas and I created this easy recipe together.
Since it needs to chill, it's a convenient make-ahead dish.

1/4 c. soybean oil
1/4 c. cider vinegar
1 T. Worcestershire sauce
2 cloves garlic, minced
salt and pepper to taste

2 14-1/2 oz. cans French-style
   green beans, drained
1 c. cherry tomatoes
1/4 c. onion, thinly sliced

For marinade, combine oil, vinegar, Worcestershire sauce, garlic, salt and pepper in a bowl. Whisk well and set aside. Place green beans in a deep bowl. Add cherry tomatoes and top with sliced onion. Pour marinade over vegetables. Cover and chill for at least 4 hours to overnight; flavor is best if chilled overnight. Serve chilled. Makes 5 to 6 servings.

You'll shed fewer tears if you peel an onion under an overhead kitchen vent. An extra-sharp knife is helpful too.

Amy's Fresh Picnic Salad

Amy Jordan
Lily, KY

This is a great side in the summer. It tastes even better the next day! If corn on the cob isn't in season, you can substitute three cups of frozen corn.

6 ears sweet corn
3 cucumbers, chopped
1 green pepper, chopped

1 red pepper, chopped
1 red onion, chopped

Make Salad Dressing ahead of time; chill. In a pot of boiling water, cook corn until tender, about 5 minutes. Rinse corn under cold running water and drain well. Slice corn kernels from ears. Combine corn and remaining vegetables in a serving bowl. Cover and refrigerate until serving time. Serve with desired amount of Salad Dressing. Makes 8 servings.

Salad Dressing:

1-1/2 c. Italian salad dressing
2 T. white vinegar
2 T. lemon juice

2 t. sugar
1 t. salt
1 t. pepper

Combine all ingredients. Chill at least 3 hours before serving.

When cutting the kernels from ears of sweet corn, stand the ear in the center of a tube cake pan. The kernels will fall neatly into the pan.

Broccoli & Tortellini Salad

Kathie Craig
Burlington, WI

*I keep the ingredients on hand to make this hearty salad.
It's easy to make on short notice. It is a favorite on rummage
sale days and after backyard water fun with the grandkids.*

19-oz. pkg. frozen cheese
   tortellini, uncooked
6 slices bacon
1/2 c. mayonnaise
1/2 c. sugar
2 t. cider vinegar

2 bunches broccoli, cut into
   flowerets
1 red onion, finely chopped
1 c. sunflower seed kernels
1 c. raisins

Cook tortellini as package directs; drain and rinse with cold water.
Meanwhile, cook bacon until crisp; drain and crumble. Stir together
mayonnaise, sugar and vinegar in a small bowl; set aside. In a large
serving bowl, combine cooked tortellini, bacon and remaining
ingredients. Add mayonnaise mixture; toss and blend. Serve
immediately, or cover and chill until serving time. Makes 10 to
12 servings.

For crunchy variety in salad toppers as well as snacking,
try Mexican pumpkin seeds, called pepitas. They're available
year 'round in the Mexican food section of most grocery stores.

Black-Eyed Pea Salad

Debi Hodges
Frederica, DE

One of my mother-in-law's favorite recipes. The longer it's chilled, the better it tastes! Canned black-eyed peas and corn make this recipe quick to fix. Use a sprinkle of celery seed instead of chopped celery, if you like.

2 16-oz. cans black-eyed peas, drained and rinsed
15-oz. can corn, drained
1/2 c. sweet onion, chopped

1/2 c. green pepper, chopped
1/2 c. celery, chopped
1 to 2 t. garlic, minced

Make Salad Dressing ahead of time; chill. In a large bowl, combine all ingredients and toss to mix. Drizzle with Salad Dressing; stir well. Cover and chill until serving time. Makes 8 servings.

Salad Dressing:

1/4 c. oil
1/4 c. sugar
2 T. cider vinegar

garlic powder, salt and pepper
to taste

Whisk together all ingredients in a small bowl. Cover and chill at least 3 hours.

Keep a cherished cookbook clean and free of spatters.
Slip it into a gallon-size plastic zipping bag before
cooking up a favorite recipe.

Bread Salad with Tomatoes

Lisa Zamfino
Fairfield, CT

I'm sure every family has a favorite recipe for using an abundance of garden tomatoes. When I shared this salad with an elderly uncle, it brought out stories of his childhood and his family that I never had the chance to get to know.

5 ripe tomatoes, cubed
salt to taste
2 t. balsamic vinegar
3 T. olive oil

2 cloves garlic, pressed
3 c. Italian bread, torn into
   bite-size pieces

Place tomatoes in a large glass bowl. Using your hands, mash tomatoes into a coarse purée. Add salt, vinegar and oil; mix well. Stir in garlic; add more salt, if desired. Just before serving, toss mixture and add bread pieces. Makes 4 servings.

Don't store tomatoes in the refrigerator...they'll quickly lose their just-picked taste. Instead, keep them on a pantry shelf or countertop, placed stem-end down.

Tomato & Watermelon Salad

Belinda Greer
Henderson, TX

This unusual salad was brought to a family reunion
and everyone loved it!

5 c. watermelon, cubed and
   seeds removed
1-1/2 lbs. ripe tomatoes, cubed
1 T. sugar
1/2 t. salt

1/2 c. red onion, quartered and
   thinly sliced
1/4 c. extra virgin olive oil
1/2 c. red wine vinegar
cracked pepper to taste

Combine watermelon and tomatoes in a large serving bowl. Sprinkle with sugar and salt; toss to coat. Let stand 15 minutes. Stir in onion, oil and vinegar. Cover and chill 2 hours. Season with pepper just before serving. Makes 8 to 10 servings.

For hearty salads in a snap, keep unopened cans of
diced tomatoes, black olives, garbanzo beans and marinated
artichokes in the fridge. They'll be chilled and ready
to toss with fresh greens at a moment's notice.

Quinoa Salad

Mary Plut
Hackettstown, NJ

This salad tastes so fresh and is a great alternative to a pasta salad! It was shared with me by a friend who is a vegetarian. My whole family loves it. When I brought some to work and shared with my co-workers, they loved it too! I will be bringing this salad to family get-togethers from now on.

4 c. water
2 c. quinoa, rinsed and uncooked
15-oz. can black olives, chopped
2 tomatoes, chopped
1 hothouse cucumber, chopped and seeded
1 green pepper, chopped
1/2 red onion, chopped

Bring water to a boil in a saucepan over medium heat; stir in quinoa. Reduce heat to medium-low. Cover and simmer until quinoa is tender and water has been absorbed, about 12 minutes. Transfer quinoa to a large bowl; cover and refrigerate about one hour. Add remaining ingredients. Pour Greek Dressing over top; fold gently until evenly mixed. Makes 8 to 10 servings.

Greek Dressing:

2/3 c. red wine vinegar
1/2 c. olive oil
1-1/4 t. garlic powder
1-1/4 t. dried oregano
1-1/4 t. dried basil
1 t. Dijon mustard
1 t. onion powder
1 t. salt
1/2 t. pepper

Whisk together all ingredients or process in a blender.

Keep cool salads chilled.
Simply nestle the salad
serving bowl into a larger
bowl filled with crushed ice.

Eat Your **Veggies!**

Rainbow Slaw

Elizabeth Quigley
League City, TX

One day as I was cooking lunch I wanted something cool to add to our meal. I had all of these ingredients on hand so I tossed together this refreshing, veggie-packed salad. It is so very good.

1/2 head green cabbage, finely
   shredded
1/2 c. red pepper, diced
1/2 c. yellow pepper, diced
2 carrots, peeled and grated

2 stalks celery, diced
salt and pepper to taste
buttermilk ranch salad dressing
   to taste

Combine all ingredients except salad dressing in a large serving bowl. Drizzle with desired amount of salad dressing; toss to coat well. Cover and refrigerate for about 30 minutes before serving. Makes 8 servings.

For the healthiest meals, choose from a rainbow of veggies...
red beets, orange sweet potatoes, yellow summer squash,
dark green kale and Brussels sprouts, purple eggplant
and blueberries. Fill your plate and eat up!

Garden Tabbouleh

Penny Heins
Choctaw, OK

*This cool dish is a big hit whenever I make it for our church potlucks!
You'll find boxes of bulghur wheat and couscous in the pasta aisle.*

1 c. bulghur wheat or couscous, uncooked
1-1/2 c. boiling water
1/4 c. lemon juice
1/4 c. extra virgin olive oil
3-1/2 t. kosher salt, divided
2 c. cherry tomatoes, halved

1 bunch green onions, minced, both white and green parts
1 hothouse cucumber, diced and seeded
1 c. fresh mint, chopped
1 c. flat-leaf parsley, chopped
1 t. pepper

Place bulghur or couscous in a large heat-safe bowl. Add boiling water, lemon juice, olive oil and 1-1/2 teaspoons salt. Stir; let stand at room temperature for about one hour. Add vegetables, herbs, pepper and remaining salt; mix well. For best flavor, cover and refrigerate for several hours before serving. Makes 10 to 12 servings.

Host an adventure potluck...a terrific way to get together
with friends old and new. Ask each guest to bring a favorite
dish from their hometown...whether that's somewhere across
the USA or even around the world. Remember to
ask everyone to bring recipe cards to share!

Eat Your Veggies!

Sweet & Sunny Kale Salad

Carla Slajchert
Tampa, FL

This is a recipe I came up with when we wanted a fresh side and didn't have much in the refrigerator. The dressing tenderizes the kale as it stands.

1 bunch fresh kale, stems
   removed
1 Gala apple, peeled, cored
   and diced

1/2 c. red onion, finely diced
1/4 c. sunflower seed kernels
1-oz. cube Parmesan cheese

Slice kale into thin ribbons. In a serving bowl, toss kale with apple, onion and sunflower seeds. Using a vegetable peeler, shave slices of Parmesan over mixture. Drizzle with Dressing; let stand for 15 to 20 minutes before serving. Makes 4 servings.

Dressing:

2 t. cider vinegar
1 t. Dijon mustard
1 t. honey

3 T. extra virgin olive oil
salt and pepper to taste

In a small bowl, combine vinegar, mustard and honey. Whisk in olive oil until combined. Season lightly with salt and pepper.

Slice a stack of kale into salad ribbons in a jiffy. Stack several leaves together and roll them up lengthwise, then slice thinly across the roll with a sharp knife.

Easy Italian New Potato Salad
Teena Hippensteel
Fort Wayne, IN

This is a quick & easy way to make a delicious salad using fresh beans and potatoes from the garden. It's ready to serve in a snap!

3/4 lb. fresh green beans,
   trimmed and halved
10 to 12 new potatoes, quartered
1/4 c. water
1/2 c. zesty Italian salad
   dressing

1/4 c. red onion, chopped
2-1/4 oz. can sliced black olives,
   drained
2 T. bacon bits

Place green beans, potatoes and water in a microwave-safe 2-quart casserole dish. Cover and microwave on high for 10 to 12 minutes, until potatoes are tender. If not using a microwave with a turntable, turn dish every 4 minutes. Drain; transfer mixture to a large glass or plastic serving bowl. Drizzle with salad dressing; toss to coat well. Gently stir in onion, olives and bacon bits. Serve immediately. Makes 8 to 10 servings.

Do you have lots of kids coming over for an after-game party? Make it easy with do-it-yourself tacos or mini pizzas... guests can add their own favorite toppings. Round out the menu with pitchers of soft drinks or lemonade and a yummy dessert pizza. Simple and fun!

Greek Barley Salad

Emily Zahn
Omaha, NE

I created this recipe to use healthy garden-fresh ingredients. If a stronger dill or garlic flavor is desired, add more to your taste.

1 c. quick or pearled barley, uncooked
3/4 c. cherry or grape tomatoes, halved
1/2 cucumber, cubed
1/4 c. red onion, sliced
1/4 c. cider vinegar

2 T. olive oil
1/2 t. granulated garlic
1/2 t. dill weed
1/4 to 1/2 t. salt
1/4 to 1/2 t. pepper
1 to 2 T. capers, drained
1/4 c. crumbled feta cheese

Prepare barley per package directions. Meanwhile, combine tomatoes, cucumber and onion in a serving bowl. Add cooked barley, vinegar, olive oil, garlic and seasonings; stir well. Add capers and feta cheese; toss to mix. May be served warm or cold. Makes 8 servings.

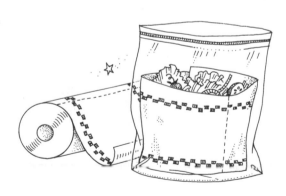

Keep salad greens crisp longer. As soon as you bring them home, transfer them to a plastic zipping bag and tuck in a moistened paper towel.

Jenny's Sweet Potato Salad

Lisa Hains
Ontario, Canada

This salad is unbelievable...so easy, yet so good! I am not a fan of sweet potatoes, but one try and I was hooked. I had to get the recipe. Try it yourself and enjoy the compliments!

3 sweet potatoes, halved
   lengthwise
1 red pepper, finely diced
1/2 c. mayonnaise, or to taste

salt and pepper to taste
Optional: hot pepper sauce
   to taste

Place sweet potatoes in a lightly greased 13"x9" baking pan. Bake, uncovered, at 350 degrees for about 45 minutes, until tender. Cool. Remove peels; cut into cubes and place in a large serving bowl. Add red pepper. Toss with mayonnaise to taste. Season with salt, pepper and hot sauce, if desired. Cover and chill until serving time. Makes 4 to 6 servings.

Make a chopped salad in seconds...no cutting board needed!
Add all the salad fixings except dressing to a big bowl,
then roll a pizza cutter back & forth over them.
Drizzle with dressing and enjoy your salad.

Eat Your Veggies!

Travis's Tree Salad

Dawn Raskiewicz
Alliance, NE

There used to be a restaurant in Scottsbluff, Nebraska that served this salad. When my son Travis was little, he called it "Tree Salad" because the broccoli looked like little trees, and the name just stuck. This salad is excellent for potluck dinners or picnics.

1 bunch broccoli, cut into
    bite-sized pieces
1 head cauliflower, cut into
    bite-sized pieces

8-oz. pkg. shredded Cheddar
    cheese
16-oz. bottle buttermilk ranch
    salad dressing

Combine broccoli and cauliflower in a large serving bowl. Add cheese and mix. Drizzle with desired amount of salad dressing; mix again. Serve, or cover and chill until serving time. Makes 8 to 10 servings.

For just-right individual servings, layer colorful salad
ingredients in one-pint Mason jars. Easy to pack for lunch...
so pretty on a picnic buffet table.

Crunchy Bacon Coleslaw

Vickie

*This delicious coleslaw is sure to be invited whenever
burgers or barbecue are on the menu.*

3/4 c. mayonnaise
1 T. sugar
1-1/2 t. cider vinegar
4 c. green cabbage, shredded
1 c. red cabbage, shredded

4 slices bacon, crisply cooked
and crumbled, or 1/2 c. real
bacon bits
1/2 c. chopped peanuts

Mix mayonnaise, sugar and vinegar in a large bowl. Add remaining ingredients; mix lightly. Cover and chill until serving time. Makes 8 to 10 servings.

Cooked vegetables that your kids won't eat may taste better
to them crunchy and raw. Serve colorful fresh veggie
slices with small cups of creamy yogurt, peanut butter
or hummus for dunking...problem solved!

Eat Your **Veggies!**

Broccoli & Pineapple Slaw

Teresa Eller
Tonganoxie, KS

I love pineapple and look for ways to include it in meals. This is one of my favorites. The crunch of the broccoli, sweetness of pineapple and the tartness of the dill just explode in your mouth with awesomeness! And it's so fast and easy to make.

12-oz. pkg. shredded broccoli
    slaw mix
8-oz. can pineapple tidbits,
    drained

1 c. mayonnaise, or to taste
1 T. dill weed
1 T. celery seed

In a large salad bowl, combine slaw mix and pineapple; toss to mix. Add remaining ingredients; toss again to coat. Cover and refrigerate until serving time. Makes 8 servings.

When you're putting away the groceries, label ingredients before refrigerating so they won't become snacks instead. Cheese cubes, fruit and veggies labeled "OK for snacking" are sure to tame appetites without upsetting your dinner plans.

Sandy's Marinated Vegetables

Sandy Coffey
Cincinnati, OH

*A great way to use farmers' market fresh veggies. Handy too...
make it ahead, then just pull it from the fridge at mealtime.*

1 head cauliflower, cut into
   bite-size pieces
2 cucumbers, sliced
2 green, red or yellow peppers,
   sliced

2 doz. mushrooms, trimmed
1/2 lb. cherry tomatoes
12-oz. bottle Italian salad
   dressing

Combine all vegetables in a large salad bowl. Drizzle with desired
amount of salad dressing; toss to coat. Cover and refrigerate overnight
to marinate. Drain before serving. Makes 6 servings.

Try this old trick for coring a head of iceberg lettuce easily.
Hold the lettuce with the core facing the kitchen counter.
Bring it down hard on the counter...the core will loosen
and can be pulled right out with your fingertips.

Family Meals
Together

Muffin Tin Meatloaves

Kathy Dean
Eau Claire, WI

These little gems cook up super fast, almost twice as fast as a traditional meatloaf.

1-1/2 lbs. lean ground beef
1 egg, lightly beaten
1 c. soft bread crumbs
1-1/2 c. zucchini, shredded

1 t. Italian seasoning
1/2 t. salt
1/4 c. catsup

In a large bowl, combine all ingredients except catsup. Mix lightly but thoroughly. Place 1/3 cup of beef mixture into each of 12 lightly greased muffin cups, pressing lightly. Spread catsup over tops. Bake at 400 degrees for 20 minutes, or until no pink remains and juices run clear. Makes 12 mini meatloaves.

To mix up a no-mess meatloaf, place all the ingredients in a large plastic zipping bag. Seal the bag and squish it until everything is well combined...then just toss the empty bag!

Not-So-Stuffed Cabbage

Michelle Bogie
Mount Morris, MI

You'll love this hearty yet easy-to-make casserole! I like to top it with homemade mild salsa for added flavor. I have made it in my slow cooker as well...it smells wonderful when coming in after a long day.

8-oz. can tomato sauce
10-3/4 oz. can tomato soup
1 T. brown sugar, packed
1/2 c. chicken broth or water
1 lb. ground beef, turkey or pork
1 onion, chopped
1 to 2 T. Worcestershire sauce
garlic powder, seasoning salt
  and pepper to taste
1 head cabbage, chopped and
  divided
4 potatoes, peeled and cubed
Optional: 1 c. mild salsa

In a bowl, stir together tomato sauce, soup, brown sugar and chicken broth or water; set aside. In a separate large bowl, combine meat, onion, Worcestershire sauce and seasonings; mix gently and set aside. In a greased 3-quart casserole dish, layer half each of cabbage and potatoes; crumble in half of meat mixture. Pour half of sauce mixture over the top. Repeat, ending with sauce mixture. If desired, pour salsa over the top. Cover and bake at 350 degrees for one hour. Uncover; bake for an additional 30 minutes. May also be prepared in a slow cooker; layer as above, cover and cook on low setting for 8 to 10 hours. Makes 6 servings.

After baking a casserole, save the aluminum foil covering. Crumble the foil into a ball and use it to scrub off any baked-on cheese or sauce in the dish.

Cavatappi & Cheese with Broccoli

Stefanie St. Pierre
South Dennis, MA

A friend gave me this recipe years ago and I adapted it for my own family. It's my most favorite mac & cheese recipe...my kids love it!

1-1/2 c. cavatappi pasta,
   uncooked
3-1/2 T. butter, divided
4-1/2 T. all-purpose flour
1/4 t. dry mustard
3/4 t. salt
1/4 t. pepper
3 c. milk

3/4 t. Worcestershire sauce
1/4 c. onion, finely chopped
8-oz. pkg. shredded sharp
   Cheddar cheese
1/2 bunch broccoli, chopped
3 T. Italian-seasoned dry bread
   crumbs

Cook pasta according to package directions; drain. Transfer pasta to a lightly greased 2-quart casserole dish; set aside. Meanwhile, in a saucepan over medium heat, melt 2 tablespoons butter; blend in flour, mustard, salt and pepper. Gradually add milk, stirring until thickened. Add Worcestershire sauce, onion and cheese; stir until cheese is melted. Pour cheese sauce over pasta and add broccoli. Stir well to combine. Melt remaining butter and toss with crumbs; sprinkle over top. Bake, uncovered, at 350 degrees for 30 minutes, or until hot and bubbly. Makes 4 to 6 servings.

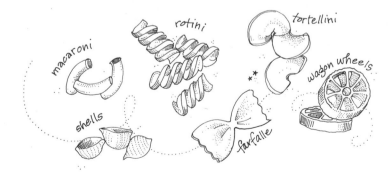

Lots of different pasta shapes like bowties, seashells and corkscrew–shaped cavatappi work well in casseroles...why not give a favorite casserole a whole new look?

Easy Chicken Stir-Fry

Randi McGee
Three Rivers, MI

I could never make a stir-fry I liked until I found this recipe. My family really likes it and it is so easy to make! Plus, with several different stir-fry veggie mixes to choose from, you'll never get bored.

2 T. oil
16-oz. pkg. frozen stir-fry
  vegetables
1 lb. cooked chicken, cubed
14-oz. can chicken broth
3-oz. pkg. chicken-flavor ramen
  noodles, broken up

2 T. cornstarch
1/3 c. cold water
salt and pepper to taste
cooked rice

Heat oil in a large, deep skillet over medium heat. Add vegetables and cook for 2 to 3 minutes, stirring often. Add chicken, broth, noodles and seasoning packets from noodles; bring to a simmer. Meanwhile, in a small bowl, add cornstarch to cold water; stir until dissolved. When noodles are tender, stir cornstarch mixture again and add to mixture in skillet. Continue cooking, stirring often, until sauce is thickened. Season with salt and pepper. Serve over cooked rice. Makes 6 servings.

Stir-frying is a terrific way to make a quick and tasty dinner. Slice veggies into equal-size pieces before you start cooking... they'll all be done to perfection at the same time.

Cheesy Zucchini & Beef Casserole

Lori Joy
Mount Vernon, IL

This hearty dish is extra delicious when you have garden-fresh veggies. My family loves it so much, though, that we even have it for Christmas dinner!

1 lb. ground beef	1 c. water
1 lb. ground pork sausage	1/2 c. shell macaroni, uncooked
2 c. zucchini, diced	2 to 3 t. dried oregano
1 c. onion, diced	2 t. salt
1 c. green pepper, diced	2 c. shredded Cheddar cheese
1 c. tomato, diced	2 c. shredded mozzarella cheese

Brown beef and sausage well in a skillet over medium heat; drain. Add vegetables, water, uncooked macaroni, oregano and salt. Bring to a boil, stirring often. Reduce heat to low. Simmer for 25 minutes, or until vegetables and macaroni are tender and liquid is almost absorbed. Stir occasionally, adding a little more water if too dry. Remove from heat; cover and let stand 10 to 15 minutes. Stir in Cheddar cheese. Spoon into a greased 13"x9" baking pan; sprinkle with mozzarella cheese. Bake, uncovered, at 375 degrees until golden and cheese is melted, 5 to 10 minutes. Makes 6 to 8 servings.

Now and then it's good to pause in our pursuit of happiness and just be happy.
– Guillaume Apollinaire

Sam's Summer Sausage Skillet
Samantha Wagner
Richmond, IN

When gardens start producing vast amounts of veggies, it's time to think of something quick & easy! Serve with a cold glass of iced tea.

10-oz. pkg. mini bowtie pasta,
  uncooked
1 T. olive oil
1 lb. mild or spicy Kielbasa
  sausage, sliced
1 onion, sliced
2 t. fresh basil, chopped

1 t. fresh rosemary, chopped
1 t. fresh oregano, chopped
1 t. garlic powder
2 zucchini, sliced
1 yellow squash, sliced
8 baby portabella mushrooms,
  sliced

Cook pasta according to package directions; drain. Meanwhile, heat olive oil in a large skillet over medium heat. Add Kielbasa, onion, herbs and garlic powder to skillet. Cook for about 5 minutes, or until sausage is beginning to brown on the edges. Add zucchini, yellow squash and mushrooms to skillet; add more seasonings, if desired. Cook until vegetables are tender, about 10 minutes. Add drained pasta to sausage mixture; stir well. Makes 4 servings.

Fill the sink with hot soapy water when you start dinner
and just toss in pans and utensils as they're used.
Clean-up will be a breeze!

Quick & Tasty Spaghetti Sauce

Marilyn Morel
Keene, NH

My husband and my boys love this tasty spaghetti sauce that's perfect for busy school nights. Just spoon it over your favorite pasta... add a salad and you have a satisfying dinner in no time at all! The sauce is great for making Sloppy Joes too.

16-oz. pkg. spaghetti or other
   pasta, uncooked
1 lb. ground beef chuck
1/2 c. onion, diced

14-1/2 oz. can diced tomatoes
14-1/2 oz. can beef broth
garlic powder, salt and pepper
   to taste

Cook pasta according to package directions; drain. Meanwhile, in a large skillet over medium heat, cook beef and onion until beef is no longer pink and onion is tender. Drain. Stir in tomatoes with juice, broth and seasonings. Bring to a boil. Reduce heat to low; cover and simmer for 10 minutes. Serve sauce over pasta. Makes 4 servings.

Tomato Butter Pasta

Cyndy DeStefano
Mercer, PA

Simple and tasty...a good budget meal for a busy weeknight. You can also add grilled chicken or cooked shrimp for a quick change.

5 T. butter, sliced
28-oz. can crushed tomatoes
1 small onion, halved

salt and pepper to taste
16-oz. pkg. angel hair pasta,
   uncooked

In a saucepan over medium heat, combine all ingredients except pasta. Cook until butter melts. Reduce heat to low. Simmer, uncovered, for 45 minutes, stirring occasionally. Shortly before serving time, cook pasta according to package directions; drain. Discard onion halves. Serve sauce over pasta. Makes 6 servings.

A pot of water for cooking pasta will boil
much quicker if it's covered with a lid.

Family Meals Together

Sassy Spaghetti Sauce

Dina Willard
Abingdon, MD

The best thing about this sassy sauce is how easy it is to prepare! Sometimes Pasta Night can be boring, so I came up with this quick version that's great for busy weeknights. Top with freshly grated Parmesan cheese for a meal that can't be beat.

32-oz. pkg. spaghetti, uncooked
2 14-1/2 oz. cans Italian-style
   diced tomatoes
7-oz. jar roasted red peppers,
   drained
7-oz. jar kalamata olives,
   drained
6-oz. jar marinated artichokes,
   drained
1/2 c. grated Parmesan cheese

Cook spaghetti according to package directions; drain and return to cooking pot. Meanwhile, in a large saucepan over medium heat, stir together remaining ingredients. Bring to a boil. Reduce heat to low; simmer for 15 minutes, stirring occasionally. Add sauce to spaghetti and mix gently. Makes 6 servings.

Cheesy Pepper Spaghetti

Shelly McBeth
Topeka, KS

This is a meal that even the pickiest eaters will love. It's simple to make in 30 minutes and can be doubled or tripled for larger groups. I have made it for many a cold fall or winter evening.

16-oz. pkg. spaghetti, uncooked
1 t. pepper
1 c. grated Parmigiano cheese
1 c. grated Pecorino Romano
   cheese

Cook spaghetti according to package directions, just until tender. Drain, reserving one cup of hot pasta water. Place hot spaghetti in a large bowl. Add pepper and cheeses. Stir gently, adding reserved pasta water in small amounts, until cheese melts and forms a creamy sauce. Serve immediately. Makes 4 servings.

Ground Beef & Kale Curry

Shannon Hildebrandt
Ontario, Canada

While on holiday, my husband and I stayed with our friends Pete and Liz, who are Kenyan nationals. They wanted us to experience Kenyan cuisine and introduced us to a version of this delicious dish. Madras curry powder is spicy, so add a little or a lot as you prefer.

1 lb. ground beef
1/2 c. onion, chopped
3 cloves garlic, minced
28-oz. can diced tomatoes
1 bunch fresh kale, torn and
    stalks removed

1/2 to 1 T. hot Madras curry
    powder
salt and pepper to taste
cooked basmati rice or
    couscous

In a large skillet over medium heat, cook beef, onion and garlic until beef is no longer pink. Stir in tomatoes with juice and kale; add desired amount of curry powder. Reduce heat to low. Cover and simmer for about 15 minutes, stirring occasionally. Season with salt and pepper. Serve over cooked rice or couscous. Makes 4 servings.

Couscous is a coarsely ground pasta made from wheat. It's a great staple that goes well with all kinds of dishes, and as fast & easy to prepare as instant rice. Look for it in the pasta aisle.

Taste of Asia Chicken

Sue Klapper
Muskego, WI

I can have this delicious dish on the table in twenty minutes.
I love it, and so do my family & friends.

20-oz. can pineapple chunks
   in juice, drained and juice
   reserved
1/2 t. ground ginger
1 lb. boneless, skinless chicken
   breasts, cubed

2 3-oz. pkgs. chicken-flavor
   ramen noodles, broken up
1/2 c. sweet-and-sour sauce
1 c. red pepper, chopped
4 green onions, thinly sliced

Set aside pineapple chunks. To reserved pineapple juice, add enough water to measure 2 cups liquid. Stir in ginger and set aside. Heat a large skillet over medium heat until hot. Lightly spray with non-stick vegetable spray. Add chicken; stir-fry for 3 to 4 minutes, stirring frequently. Add pineapple juice mixture to skillet; bring to a boil. Add noodles and seasoning packets from noodles. Bring to a boil; reduce heat to low. Simmer for 3 minutes, or until noodles are tender and most of liquid is absorbed. Add sweet-and-sour sauce, red pepper, green onions and reserved pineapple chunks to skillet; heat through. Serve immediately. Makes 6 servings.

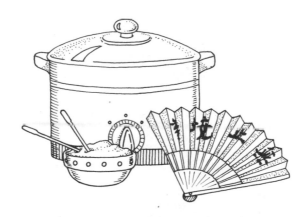

Chicken thighs are juicy, flavorful and budget-friendly.
Feel free to substitute them in most recipes that
call for chicken breasts.

Chicken Quesadillas

Charlotte Smith
Alexandria, PA

These quesadillas are very tasty and quick. Feel free to add or subtract ingredients to your liking.

1 T. oil
1-1/2 c. cooked chicken breast, diced or shredded
1/2 c. green pepper, diced
1/2 c. red pepper, diced
1/2 c. green onions, sliced
1 c. salsa

1/2 t. pepper, or to taste
Optional: 1 t. chili powder
6 to 8 large flour tortillas
1 c. shredded Monterey Jack or Cheddar cheese
Garnish: sour cream, additional salsa

Heat oil in a large saucepan over medium heat. Add chicken, red and green peppers and green onions. Sauté, keeping peppers and onions slightly crisp. Drain; add salsa, pepper and chili powder, if using. Mix well and heat through. Spoon 2 heaping tablespoons of chicken mixture onto one-half of each tortilla; top with 2 to 3 teaspoons cheese and fold over other half of tortilla. Cut in half, forming 2 wedges each. Add wedges to a non-stick skillet over medium-high heat. Cook until lightly golden on both sides and cheese is melted. Serve warm, topped with sour cream and remaining salsa. Makes 6 to 8 servings.

Feeding a crowd? Serve festive Mexican, Italian or Chinese-style dishes that everybody loves. They usually feature rice or pasta, so they're filling yet budget-friendly. The theme makes it a snap to put together the menu and table decorations too.

Stuffed Poblano Peppers

Renee Hopfer
Stokesdale, NC

*My husband loves chiles relleno and orders them every time
we go out for Mexican food. I wanted to make a similar type
of dish at home and came up with this recipe.*

6.8-oz. pkg. Spanish rice-
   flavored rice vermicelli mix
10-oz. can diced tomatoes with
   green chiles
1 lb. lean ground beef
salt and pepper to taste

8-oz. pkg. shredded Mexican-
   blend cheese, divided
6 large poblano peppers
Garnish: tortilla chips, sour
   cream, salsa

Prepare Spanish rice mix according package directions. Before turning
rice mix down to simmer, stir in tomatoes with chiles. Meanwhile, in
a large skillet over medium heat, brown beef and drain. Season beef
with salt and pepper. When rice is done, add rice to beef along with
1/2 cup shredded cheese. Mix well. Slice down one side of each
pepper; remove stem caps and seeds. Fill peppers generously with rice
mixture. Arrange peppers in a greased 2-quart casserole dish. Cover
with aluminum foil. Bake at 350 degrees for 35 to 45 minutes,
checking after 25 minutes, until peppers are tender. Uncover; top
peppers with cheese and re-cover with foil. Bake an additional 5 to
7 minutes, until cheese is melted. Serve with tortilla chips, sour cream
and salsa. Makes 6 servings.

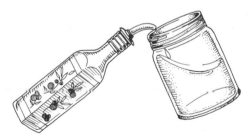

Shake up a tasty dressing for lettuce, tomato and avocado
salad...terrific alongside spicy Mexican dishes. In a covered jar,
combine 3 tablespoons olive oil, 2 tablespoons lime juice,
1/4 teaspoon dry mustard and 1/2 teaspoon salt.
Cover and shake until well blended.

Arlene's Chuck Wagon Skillet

Arlene Bennett
Graham, WA

*I've been making this dish for 60 years. I used to serve it
for lunch when my kids were little. Very good!*

2 T. butter
1/4 c. onion, chopped
1 lb. ground beef
1 c. celery, chopped
salt to taste

1 t. pepper
2 c. shredded Cheddar cheese
2 c. wide egg noodles, uncooked
1/4 c. water
14-1/2 oz. can stewed tomatoes

Melt butter in a skillet over medium heat; cook onion until tender. Add
beef and celery to skillet. Cook until beef is browned; drain. Season
with salt and pepper. Layer with cheese and uncooked noodles. Pour
water and tomatoes with juice over all. Cover skillet; cook until
steaming. Reduce heat to low. Simmer, covered, for 35 minutes.
Makes 6 servings.

Oops! If a simmering skillet or soup pot begins to burn
on the bottom, all is not lost. Spoon it into another pan,
being careful not to scrape up the scorched food on
the bottom. The burnt taste usually won't linger.

Nacho Skillet Dinner

Allison Steele
Mount Crawford, VA

A great one-dish meal!

1-1/2 lbs. ground beef
1 c. green pepper, chopped
1/2 c. onion, chopped
2 t. garlic powder
15-oz. can kidney beans,
   drained and rinsed

14-1/2 oz. can diced tomatoes
1-1/4 oz. pkg. taco seasoning
   mix
1 c. shredded Mexican-style
   cheese
tortilla chips

Brown beef in a skillet over medium heat; drain and set beef aside. To same skillet, add green pepper, onion and garlic powder. Cook until vegetables are soft, about 8 minutes. Stir in beef, kidney beans, tomatoes with juice and taco seasoning. Cook over medium heat until bubbly, about 5 minutes. Sprinkle with cheese. Reduce heat to low; cover and cook until cheese melts, about 5 minutes. To serve, arrange tortilla chips on dinner plates; spoon beef mixture over tortilla chips. Makes 6 servings.

Try using a little less ground beef in your favorite recipe.
Add a few more veggies...there's a good chance that
no one will even notice!

Spanish Hot Dog Sauce

Cheryl Panning
Wabash, IN

This is great for a cookout or any gathering of friends. I make it for our euchre group and they love it. Steam hot dogs, put them on fresh buns and fill with sauce...it is better than any take-out meal! This freezes well if you have any left over. It really is an exceptional sauce. Be prepared to hand out the recipe!

2 lbs. ground beef
1/2 c. onion, diced
8-oz. can tomato sauce
1 c. catsup
2 T. brown sugar, packed
2 to 3 T. chili powder

1/2 t. red pepper flakes
1/2 t. garlic salt
1 t. salt
1 t. pepper
1/8 t. cinnamon

Brown beef with onion in a large deep skillet over medium heat; drain. Stir in remaining ingredients; bring to a boil. Reduce heat to low. Cook until thickened, stirring often, about 20 minutes. Makes about 20 servings.

Get rid of tomato sauce stains on a plastic storage container by rubbing the stain with a damp cloth dipped in baking soda. You can also try filling the stained container with water and dropping in one or two foaming denture cleaning tablets. Wait 20 minutes and rinse.

Beef & Shell Stuff

Leslie Harvie
Simpsonville, SC

I found the original recipe for this dish written in the back of one of my mom's cookbooks. It quickly became one of my teenage son Tyler's favorite meals. When asked what we should have for dinner, he often answers, "Beef & Shell Stuff!" Sometimes I double the recipe...teenage boys can eat a lot!

1 onion, chopped
3 cloves garlic, minced
1 T. olive oil
1 lb. ground beef
2 14-1/2 oz. cans stewed
   tomatoes
8-oz. pkg. shell macaroni,
   uncooked

1-3/4 c. water
1 t. Italian seasoning
salt and pepper to taste
Optional: grated Parmesan
   cheese

In a large skillet over medium heat, sauté onion and garlic in olive oil until translucent; drain. Add beef and cook until browned; drain. Stir in tomatoes with juice and uncooked macaroni. Pour water over beef mixture; stir in seasonings. Bring to a boil. Reduce heat to low. Cover and simmer until macaroni is tender and liquid is absorbed. Sprinkle individual servings with Parmesan cheese, if desired. Makes 6 servings.

The flavor of freshly shredded Parmesan cheese can't be beat in pasta and veggie dishes. To keep a chunk of hard cheese fresh longer, rub softened butter over the cut sides, tuck the cheese into a plastic zipping bag and refrigerate.

Penne with Asparagus & Peppers

Susan Griffith
Columbus, OH

*A flavorful veggie-packed dish that you'll love. If you'd like
a heartier meal, just add some cooked, cubed chicken.*

2 yellow peppers
2 red peppers
1 lb. asparagus, trimmed and
   cut into 2-inch pieces
1 t. garlic, minced
1-1/2 c. chicken broth
12-oz. pkg. penne pasta,
   uncooked

1-1/2 T. fresh thyme, minced
2 T. butter, sliced
2/3 c. grated Parmigiano
   Reggiano cheese, divided
1 t. kosher salt
1/8 t. pepper

Char peppers; peel, dice and set aside. In a large skillet over medium
heat, cover asparagus with lightly salted water. Bring to a boil; cook
until asparagus begins to soften, about one minute. Drain. Add peppers
and garlic to skillet; cook and stir for one minute. Add chicken broth
and bring to a boil; remove skillet from heat. Cook pasta according to
package directions, just until tender; drain. Return skillet to medium
heat; add cooked pasta and thyme. Simmer, stirring often, for 5 to
7 minutes. Stir in butter, 1/3 cup cheese, salt and pepper. Transfer to
a serving bowl; top with remaining cheese. Serves 4 to 6.

Char sweet peppers to give them a delicious, smoky taste.
Arrange peppers on an aluminum foil-lined broiler pan. Broil
for 20 to 25 minutes, until peppers are blackened and soft,
turning them with tongs every five minutes. Cool.
The skins will remove easily; discard the seeds also.

Chicken Tortellini Stovetop Casserole

Carolyn Deckard
Bedford, IN

This is a fast and easy meal that everyone in my family likes.

2 9-oz. pkgs. refrigerated
   cheese tortellini, uncooked
4 c. broccoli and/or cauliflower,
   cut into bite-size flowerets
14-1/2 oz. can Italian-style
   diced tomatoes

1/2 c. tomato pesto sauce
9-oz. pkg. frozen roasted or
   grilled chicken breast strips,
   thawed
Optional: shaved Parmesan
   cheese

Cook tortellini according to package directions, adding broccoli and/or cauliflower the last 3 minutes of cooking. Drain; return tortellini and vegetables to pasta pot. Stir in tomatoes with juice, pesto and chicken. Cook over low heat, stirring occasionally, for 5 to 10 minutes, until heated through. Garnish with Parmesan cheese, if desired. Makes 4 servings.

Spray the panels of a door with chalkboard paint and let dry... a clever chalkboard the whole family will love! It's just right for sharing what's on the menu tonight.

One-Pan Roast Chicken Dinner

Kathy Harris
Valley Center, KS

This is my go-to recipe whenever I need a fast, easy, nutritious dinner. The oven does all the work...I love how crisp the chicken gets and it's not even fried! Trust me, it goes together in no time.

6 T. olive oil, divided
2 lemons, divided
4 cloves garlic, minced
1 t. kosher salt
1/2 t. pepper

3/4 lb. fresh green beans,
   trimmed
8 new redskin potatoes,
   quartered
4 chicken thighs or breasts

Coat a 13"x9" baking pan or cast-iron skillet with one tablespoon olive oil. Thinly slice one lemon; arrange lemon slices in pan in a single layer and set aside. Squeeze juice from remaining lemon. In a large bowl, combine remaining oil, lemon juice, garlic, salt and pepper; add green beans and toss to coat. With a slotted spoon, arrange beans on top of lemon slices. Add potatoes to oil mixture; toss to coat. With slotted spoon, arrange potatoes around edge of pan, on top of beans. Add chicken to oil mixture and coat thoroughly. Place chicken in pan, skin-side up. Drizzle any remaining oil mixture over chicken. Bake, uncovered, at 450 degrees for 50 minutes, or until chicken juices run clear. Remove chicken to a plate; keep warm. Return beans and potatoes to oven for another 10 minutes, or until potatoes are fork-tender. Serve each chicken piece with some of the beans and potatoes. Makes 4 servings.

Large bottles of olive oil stay freshest in the fridge. Pour a little into a squeeze bottle to keep in the cupboard for everyday use.

Mimi's Stuffed Pork Chops

Mori Green
Conroe, TX

*I love making this recipe for Sunday lunch. It is one of
my family's favorites.*

6-oz. pkg. pork or chicken-
  flavored stuffing mix
1 c. yellow onion, chopped
1 red pepper, chopped
1/4 c. butter, sliced

6 to 10 boneless pork chops,
  1-inch thick
2 12-oz. jars turkey gravy,
  or 3 c. homemade gravy

Prepare stuffing mix as package directs. Meanwhile, in a small skillet
over medium heat, cook onion and red pepper in butter until onion is
tender. Stir onion mixture into prepared stuffing. With a sharp knife,
cut into the side of each pork chop to form a pocket. Scoop 2 spoonfuls
of stuffing into each pork chop; fasten with a wooden toothpick in each
end. Place stuffed pork chops in a 2-quart casserole dish; spoon any
remaining stuffing around pork chops. Spoon gravy over pork chops
and stuffing. Cover and bake at 350 degrees for one to 1-1/4 hours,
until pork chops are tender. Makes 6 to 10 servings.

For a brand-new meal your family will love, pizza-fy those
leftovers! Top a ready-to-bake pizza crust with sliced baked
chicken or grilled steak, fresh or cooked veggies and whatever
sounds good to you. Finish with a sprinkle of cheese and bake
until hot and bubbly, about ten minutes at 400 degrees. Yummy!

Meal-in-One Meaty Vegetable Skillet

Linda Smith
Columbia, MO

This is such an easy-to-make meal. Whenever I got home late, I could toss this together very quickly. I still make this dish often and my family loves it.

1 lb. ground turkey or beef
1/2 c. onion, chopped
1 t. oil
14-1/2 oz. can diced tomatoes
  with basil, garlic & oregano

15-1/2 oz. can chili beans
  in sauce
1 to 2 zucchini, diced
1/4 c. dill pickle, chopped
1/2 t. pepper

In a skillet over medium heat, brown turkey or beef and onion in oil. Drain; stir in tomatoes with sauce and remaining ingredients. Simmer, uncovered, for 5 to 10 minutes, until zucchini is tender. Makes 6 servings.

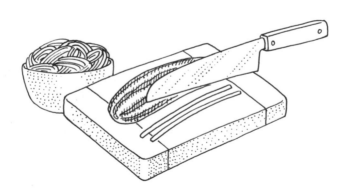

For a healthy change from regular pasta, make "noodles" from zucchini or summer squash. Cut the squash into long, thin strips, steam lightly or sauté in a little olive oil and toss with your favorite pasta sauce.

Skillet Barbecued Chicken

Marian Forck
Chamois, MO

When I was growing up, Mom would make delicious
chicken this way. It was so good to enjoy barbecue
even when we couldn't grill outdoors.

1/3 c. catsup
1/4 c. water
2 T. brown sugar, packed
2 T. cider vinegar

2 T. oil
1 T. Worcestershire sauce
1/4 t. pepper
2 lbs. chicken pieces

In a large skillet over medium heat, combine all ingredients except chicken; stir until well combined. Add chicken; turn to coat with sauce. Cook for 35 to 45 minutes, turning occasionally, until chicken is evenly golden and juices run clear. Makes 4 servings.

When frying chicken or browning beef for stew, you'll get the best results if the pan isn't overcrowded. Use an extra large skillet or cook in two batches.

Buffalo Chicken Fingers

Jessica Kraus
Delaware, OH

These spicy chicken strips are great! You can adjust the seasoning to the level of heat you want. Any leftovers are great to top a salad...with celery and blue cheese dressing, of course!

1/4 c. all-purpose flour
1 t. garlic powder, divided
1 t. cayenne pepper, divided
1/2 t. salt, divided
3/4 c. dry bread crumbs

2 egg whites, beaten
1 T. water
4 boneless, skinless chicken
   breasts, cut into finger-sized
   strips

In a plastic zipping bag, mix together flour, 1/2 teaspoon garlic powder, 1/2 teaspoon cayenne pepper and 1/4 teaspoon salt. On a plate, mix bread crumbs with remaining seasonings. In a shallow bowl, beat egg whites with water. Add chicken strips to bag and shake to coat. Dip chicken in egg mixture, then roll in bread crumb mixture. Arrange chicken on a baking sheet that has been sprayed with non-stick vegetable spray. Bake at 400 degrees for about 8 minutes. Turn chicken over. Bake an additional 8 minutes, or until golden and chicken juices run clear. Makes 8 servings.

Take it easy on alternate Friday nights...arrange for a friendly dinner swap! One week, you make a double batch of a favorite casserole and deliver one to a friend. Next week, she returns the favor. You're sure to discover some great new recipes while gaining a little free time too.

Carol's Crispy Baked Chicken

Carol Brownridge
Georgetown, ON

This is a very easy chicken recipe that I like to make for Sunday night dinners. The crisp skin really sets this recipe apart!

4 chicken leg quarters	1 t. onion powder
1/2 c. soy sauce, divided	1 t. salt
1 t. garlic powder	1/2 t. pepper

Arrange chicken leg quarters on an aluminum foil-lined 13"x9" baking pan. With your fingers, loosen skin on chicken, making a flap, but making sure skin stays attached at most points. Brush half the soy sauce under the chicken skin. In a cup, mix seasonings together. Sprinkle half the seasoning mixture on chicken under the skin; rub into chicken. Brush remaining soy sauce over both sides of chicken; sprinkle with remaining seasoning mixture. Bake, uncovered, at 375 degrees for one hour. Increase oven temperature to 400 degrees and bake for 15 minutes more. Remove from oven; let stand for 5 minutes before serving. Makes 4 servings.

Try barley pilaf instead of rice or noodles on the side. Simply prepare quick-cooking barley with chicken or vegetable broth instead of water. Season with a little chopped onion and dried parsley. Filling, healthful and tasty!

Beef Stroganoff

Joan Thamsen
Middletown, NY

This is a quick weeknight meal that has always been a hit in our house. It makes a great presentation and looks much more difficult than it is. Guests will be impressed as well.

1/2 c. onion, finely chopped
2 T. butter, sliced
1 lb. beef top round or London
    broil, thinly sliced
paprika, salt and pepper to taste

1 c. sour cream
1 T. all-purpose flour
1 T. hot water
cooked rice or egg noodles

In a skillet over medium heat, sauté onion in butter until lightly golden. Add beef; sauté until browned on both sides. Sprinkle with seasonings. Reduce heat to low; cover skillet. Mix together sour cream, flour and water; stir into beef mixture. Simmer, covered, for about 30 minutes, stirring occasionally. To serve, ladle over cooked rice or egg noodles. Makes 4 servings.

Save extra cooked noodles for another meal. Place them in a plastic zipping bag, toss with a little olive oil to coat noodles, close tightly and refrigerate for three to four days. To reheat, pour into a metal colander and immerse colander in a pot of boiling water for one minute. Drain and serve.

Bacon–Gouda Mac & Cheese

Becky Drees
Pittsfield, MA

For all you bacon lovers out there!

16-oz. pkg. favorite short pasta,
   uncooked
6 slices bacon
1 sweet onion, diced

salt and pepper to taste
1 c. whipping cream
1 c. smoked Gouda cheese,
   grated

Cook pasta according to package directions; drain. Meanwhile, in a skillet over medium heat, cook bacon until crisp. Remove bacon to a paper towel to drain; chop coarsely. Reserve one tablespoon drippings in skillet. Add onion to drippings. Cook over medium heat for about 5 minutes, until translucent and slightly soft. Season onion with salt and pepper. Return bacon to skillet; stir in cream. Simmer over medium-high heat for several minutes, until mixture has reduced and thickened slightly. Turn off the heat and add cheese; stir until cheese melts. Add cooked pasta and stir until coated in sauce. Season with additional salt and pepper, as needed. Makes 6 servings.

Prefer to shred cheese yourself? Place the wrapped block of cheese in the freezer for 15 minutes...it will just glide across the grater! Use right away, or place in a plastic zipping bag to refrigerate (up to three days) or freeze. Two cups shredded cheese equals an 8-ounce package.

Gram's Upper-Crust Chicken

Sandy Coffey
Cincinnati, OH

An easy recipe that my kids and grandkids enjoy. I always have extra cooked chicken on hand, as most folks like some kind of chicken dish. Easy to put together...since it needs to chill for a few hours, just tuck it in the fridge early in the afternoon and go about your day. Serve with your favorite veggies and hot buttered rolls.

8 slices bread
2 c. cooked chicken, cubed
1 c. celery, chopped
2 c. shredded Cheddar cheese,
    divided

2 eggs, beaten
1 c. mayonnaise
1/2 t. salt
1/2 t. poultry seasoning
2 c. milk

Trim crusts from bread. Cut crusts into small cubes; set aside bread slices. In a bowl, mix crust cubes, chicken, celery and 1-3/4 cups cheese. Spoon into a greased 2-quart casserole dish. Cut bread slices into quarters and arrange on top of chicken mixture; set aside. In a separate bowl, whisk together eggs, mayonnaise and seasonings. Gradually add milk, mixing well. Spoon over bread and chicken mixture. Sprinkle remaining cheese on top. Cover and refrigerate for 2 to 4 hours. Uncover; bake at 375 degrees for 30 to 40 minutes, until puffed and golden. Makes 4 servings.

Take time to share family stories and traditions with your kids over the dinner table! A cherished family recipe can be a super conversation starter.

Mustard Chicken

Joy Collins
Vestavia, AL

This dish is easy and delicious! If I haven't made it for awhile, my husband will ask for it. It's easy to double or even triple if you're hosting a crowd or going to a potluck.

1/2 c. mayonnaise
1/2 c. butter, melted and
   slightly cooled
3 T. mustard

6-oz. pkg. herb-flavored
   stuffing mix
8 boneless, skinless chicken
   breasts

Mix together mayonnaise, butter and mustard in a shallow bowl. Place dry stuffing mix in a separate shallow bowl. Add chicken to mayonnaise mixture; coat well. Dip chicken into stuffing mix and press on both sides to coat. Arrange chicken in a lightly greased 13"x9" baking pan. Bake, covered, at 350 degrees for one hour. Uncover; bake for another 30 minutes, or until chicken juices run clear. Makes 8 servings.

Out of bread crumbs for a casserole? Substitute crushed herb-flavored stuffing mix instead and it will be just as tasty.

Crustless Zucchini Pie

Laurel Perry
Loganville, GA

This super-easy pie is a great way to enjoy fresh veggies from your garden or the neighborhood farmers' market. It's a terrific light supper or lunch, even a good brunch dish.

4 eggs, beaten
1/4 c. oil
salt and pepper to taste
1 c. biscuit baking mix
1 t. baking powder
1-1/2 c. zucchini, sliced

1-1/2 c. yellow squash, sliced
1/2 c. sweet onion, chopped
1 to 2 ripe tomatoes, sliced
1/4 c. grated Parmesan cheese
3 T. fresh parsley, chopped

In a large bowl, whisk together eggs, oil, salt and pepper. Stir in biscuit mix and baking powder until moistened. Gently fold in zucchini, summer squash and onion. Pour into a lightly greased 9" deep-dish pie plate. Arrange tomato slices on top; sprinkle with Parmesan cheese and parsley. Bake at 350 degrees until puffed and golden, about 30 to 40 minutes. Cut into wedges; serve warm. Makes 6 servings.

For the tastiest results, reduce the oven temperature by 25 degrees when using glass or dark pie plates or baking pans...they retain more heat than shiny pans.

Zesty Eggplant Parmesan
Joanna Nicoline-Haughey
Berwyn, PA

Whether you grow your own eggplant or take a trip to your local farm market, you will enjoy this super-easy, tasty dish!

2 eggplants, halved lengthwise
24-oz. jar pasta sauce, divided
1/4 c. extra virgin olive oil
1/2 c. seasoned dry bread
   crumbs
1/2 c. grated Parmesan cheese,
   divided
pepper to taste
8-oz. pkg. shredded mozzarella
   cheese

Cut eggplants into 1/2-inch slices; set aside. Spread 1-1/2 cups pasta sauce in a lightly greased 13"x9" baking pan. Arrange eggplant slices over sauce, overlapping slices. Drizzle with olive oil. Sprinkle with bread crumbs and half of the Parmesan cheese; season with pepper. Top with remaining sauce and Parmesan cheese. Bake, uncovered, at 450 degrees for 45 minutes. Top with mozzarella cheese. Return to oven for 3 minutes, or until cheese is melted. Makes 6 servings.

Warm garlic bread can't be beat! Mix 1/2 cup melted butter and 2 teaspoons minced garlic; spread over a split loaf of Italian bread. Sprinkle with chopped fresh parsley. Bake at 350 degrees for 8 minutes, or until hot, then broil briefly, until golden. Cut into generous slices.

Tuna Spaghetti

Debbi Luckett
Mechanicsburg, OH

This is a budget-friendly dish and it's delicious! You would never guess there's tuna in the sauce.

16-oz. pkg spaghetti, uncooked
1 T. oil
1/2 c. onion, chopped
1/4 c. green pepper, chopped
28-oz. can tomato purée
1 c. water
1 stalk celery, thinly sliced
1/4 t. dried basil

1/4 t. dried oregano
1 t. salt
1/8 t. pepper
6-1/2 oz. can chunk tuna,
 drained and flaked
8-oz. can tomato sauce
1/2 c. fresh parsley, chopped

Cook spaghetti according to package directions; drain. Meanwhile, heat oil in a large saucepan over medium heat. Add onion and green pepper; sauté until tender, about 3 minutes. Add tomato purée, water, celery and seasonings to saucepan; bring to a boil. Reduce heat to low. Simmer, uncovered, about 30 minutes, stirring occasionally. Stir in tuna, tomato sauce and parsley; cook just until bubbly. To serve, ladle sauce over cooked spaghetti. Makes 6 servings.

A Lazy Susan is oh-so handy when storing lots of jars and cans in the pantry. Give it a quick spin to bring the item you want right to the front of the cupboard.

Stovetop Tuna Casserole

Sonya Labbe
Los Angeles, CA

We like tuna casserole, but there are days that I just don't want to use the oven. This casserole is very tasty and is a breeze to make.

8-oz. pkg. elbow macaroni,
   uncooked
6-1/2 oz. container semi-soft
   light garlic & herb cheese
1/2 c. milk, divided

2 12-1/4 oz. cans solid white
   tuna in water, drained and
   broken up
2 t. dill weed

Cook macaroni according to package directions. Drain; return macaroni to pan. Add cheese and 1/4 cup milk to macaroni. Cook and stir over medium heat until cheese is melted and macaroni is coated, adding remaining milk as needed for a creamy consistency. Gently fold in tuna and dill; heat through. Makes 4 servings.

Garden-fresh vegetables are delicious steamed and topped with pats of chive butter. To make, blend 1/4 cup softened butter with 2 tablespoons chopped fresh chives, one teaspoon lemon zest and a little salt & pepper.

Pesto Tilapia

Peggy Borrok
Lafayette, LA

This is so easy, quick and tasty. Even my picky kids love it!

6 tilapia fillets, thawed if frozen
2 T. olive oil
salt and pepper to taste
6 T. basil pesto sauce

14-1/2 oz. can petite diced
  tomatoes, drained
1-1/2 c. shredded mozzarella
  cheese

Arrange fish fillets on an aluminum foil-lined baking sheet. Drizzle with oil and sprinkle with salt and pepper. Spread one tablespoon pesto over each fillet; divide tomatoes evenly among fillets and place 1/4 cup cheese on top of each fillet. Bake, uncovered, at 400 degrees for 12 to 15 minutes, until fish flakes easily with a fork. Makes 6 servings.

Salsa Halibut

Sonya Labbe
Los Angeles, CA

One evening when we didn't have much on hand, I came up with this tasty recipe. We had a very nice meal in a jiffy! Serve with couscous and steamed green beans for an easy and fast meal.

1 lb. halibut steaks, 3/4-inch
  thick, thawed if frozen
2 T. Dijon mustard

1/2 c. chunky roasted vegetable
  or tomato salsa

Pat fish dry. Arrange fish in a lightly greased shallow 2-quart rectangular casserole dish. Bake, uncovered, at 450 degrees for 6 to 9 minutes, until fish flakes easily with a fork. Drain off any liquid. Spread mustard over fish; spoon salsa over mustard. Return to oven for 2 to 3 minutes, until heated through. Makes 4 servings.

For fresh-tasting fish, place thawed fillets in a shallow dish and cover with milk. Soak for 20 minutes, then pat dry.

Greek Salmon

Terri Stanifer
Stanton, TN

I came up with this simple microwave recipe when we were trying to eat healthier and add more fish to our diet. For best results, the salmon pieces should be as close to the same size as possible.

1 lb. salmon, cut into
    4 serving-size pieces

1/4 c. extra virgin olive oil
3 T. Greek seasoning

Brush fish with olive oil, coating all sides. Sprinkle with seasoning. Arrange fish in a microwave-safe dish. Cover and microwave at 50% power for 15 minutes, or until fish flakes easily with a fork. Let stand 5 minutes before serving. Makes 4 servings.

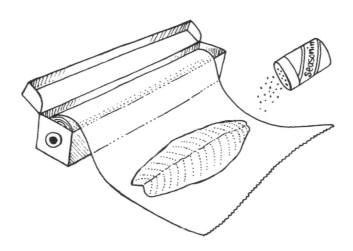

Bake fish fillets in parchment paper for a delicious dinner with no fuss. Season fish and place on a sheet of parchment paper. Fold up the sides and crimp to make a tight package; place on a baking pan. Bake as usual, then slice open package and serve fish with its juices. Afterwards, just toss away the paper.

Linguine & Red Clam Sauce

Sandy Ann Ward
Anderson, IN

*This dish is full of flavor and so easy to prepare. If you prefer,
you can use three ten-ounce cans of whole baby clams, drained.*

16-oz. pkg. linguine pasta,
  uncooked
1/4 c. olive oil
1/4 c. butter, sliced
2 onions, chopped
2 cloves garlic, chopped
28-oz. can petite diced tomatoes

14-1/2 oz. can crushed tomatoes
1/4 c. fresh parsley, chopped
  and divided
4 6-1/2 oz. cans chopped
  clams, drained
Garnish: grated Parmesan
  cheese

Cook pasta according to package directions; drain. Combine olive oil
and butter in a large saucepan over medium-low heat. Add onions and
garlic; sauté until onions are tender, about 5 minutes. Stir in both cans
of tomatoes with juice and 2 tablespoons parsley. Reduce heat to low.
Simmer, covered, for about 25 minutes. Stir in clams; simmer an
additional 5 minutes. Ladle sauce over cooked pasta; sprinkle with
remaining parsley. Serve with Parmesan cheese. Makes 6 servings.

Laughter really is the best medicine! Studies show that
time spent laughing provides all kinds of health benefits...
it can even burn extra calories. So be sure to share funny
stories and the kids' latest jokes everyday over dinner.

Shrimp Irene

Irene Robinson
Cincinnati, OH

A sweet & simple dish...perfect for nights when it's just the two of you, yet easy to double when there are guests for dinner.

1/4 c. butter, sliced
1/8 t. lemon juice
1/2 t. garlic powder
1/2 lb. uncooked medium
    shrimp, cleaned and
    tails removed

1/4 c. white wine or chicken
    broth
2 T. dry bread crumbs
cooked rice

Combine butter, lemon juice and garlic powder in a skillet over medium heat. Add shrimp and sauté for about 3 minutes, until pink. Add wine or broth; simmer about 3 minutes. Sprinkle in bread crumbs. Cook and stir until sauce has thickened and crumbs make a light coating. Serve shrimp with sauce from skillet over cooked rice. Makes 2 servings.

Mix up a bowl of pineapple coleslaw in a jiffy. Combine a package of shredded coleslaw mix and your favorite coleslaw dressing, adding dressing to taste. Stir in some drained pineapple tidbits for a sweet twist.

Parmesan Salmon Bake with Penne

Karen McCann
Marion, OH

I originally found this on a recipe website and our family fell in love with this dish. We like cheese so we add a little bit more.

16-oz. pkg. penne pasta, uncooked
10 T. butter, divided
2 c. half-and-half
1/2 c. grated Parmesan cheese
1/4 t. nutmeg
salt and pepper to taste

15-oz. can salmon, drained and flaked, bones and skin removed
1 T. fresh parsley, finely chopped
Garnish: additional grated Parmesan cheese

Cook pasta according to package directions. Drain; transfer pasta to a 13"x9" baking pan coated with one tablespoon butter. Toss pasta with one tablespoon butter to coat well; set aside. Meanwhile, in a saucepan over medium heat, whisk together remaining butter, half-and-half, cheese and nutmeg until sauce thickens. Season with salt and pepper. Pour sauce over pasta; add salmon and parsley and mix well. Bake, uncovered, at 425 degrees for 15 to 20 minutes, until hot and bubbly. Serve with additional Parmesan cheese. Makes 8 servings.

A full pantry makes it so easy to toss together all kinds of tasty meals in a jiffy. Stock the cupboard with cans of chicken, tuna, salmon and other canned meats along with packages of pasta and rice...no more last-minute trips to the grocery store.

Butter–Baked Flounder

Irene Robinson
Cincinnati, OH

A fast and wonderful fish recipe that can be made with other kinds of fish too. We enjoy this often during Lent.

1/4 c. butter, melted
1 t. onion, minced
2 t. fresh parsley, minced
1 t. salt
1/2 t. pepper

1 T. lemon juice
1 t. Worcestershire sauce
1-1/2 lbs. flounder fillets,
    thawed if frozen

In a shallow dish, combine all ingredients except fish. Dip fillets into butter mixture. Arrange in a lightly greased shallow 13"x9" baking pan. Spoon remaining butter mixture over fish. Bake, uncovered, at 375 degrees for 25 to 30 minutes, until fish flakes easily with a fork. Makes 6 servings.

Change the flavor of a favorite fish dish just by trying a different type of fish in the recipe. Mild-flavored cod, flounder and haddock can all be swapped in recipes.

Creamed Chicken

Megan Simpson
Smithsburg, MD

My mom calls this recipe "Decontructed Chicken Pot Pie." It is yummy on a cold winter day. Serve over whatever you have on hand...baked potatoes, waffles, English muffins, cooked rice or pasta are all good choices. Tastes wonderful served with cranberry sauce!

1/4 c. butter, sliced
1 onion, chopped
1 green pepper, chopped
3 stalks celery, chopped
1/4 c. all-purpose flour
1 c. milk
2 c. chicken broth

1/2 t. herbes de Provence or
    dried thyme
1/8 t. pepper
2 c. cooked chicken, diced
2 15-oz. cans mixed vegetables,
    drained
toast slices or cooked rice

Melt butter in a large non-stick saucepan over medium heat. Add onion, green pepper and celery; sauté until soft, about 5 minutes. Remove from heat. Stir in flour, mixing well. Add milk, broth and seasonings; return saucepan to medium heat. Stir constantly until mixture comes to a boil. Stir in chicken and mixed vegetables. Reduce heat to low; simmer for 15 to 20 minutes. To serve, spoon over toast slices or cooked rice. Makes 6 servings.

Not sure if the spices in your spice cupboard are still fresh and flavorful? Open the container and hold it at chin level...if you can't detect the aroma, your spice is past its prime.

Creamy Ham & Biscuits

Maggie Antonelli
Vancouver, WA

I created this recipe while realizing I didn't have the chicken for Chicken à la King. Now my family cannot get enough of this! It has become a family staple.

1/2 c. butter, sliced
1-1/2 c. frozen peas & carrots
4-oz. can sliced mushrooms,
   drained and liquid reserved
1/2 c. all-purpose flour
1 t. salt
1/2 t. pepper

1 t. garlic powder
1-1/2 c. milk
1-1/4 c. very hot water
3/4 lb. cooked ham, diced
4-oz. jar diced pimentos, drained
16-oz. tube refrigerated jumbo
   buttermilk biscuits

Melt butter in a large skillet over medium heat. Add peas & carrots and mushrooms; cook for 5 minutes. Add flour and seasonings; stir continually until bubbly. Remove skillet from heat. Stirring well, gradually add milk, then reserved mushroom liquid, then hot water. Return skillet to medium heat. Bring mixture to a boil; continue to boil and stir for one minute. Stir in ham and pimentos. Spoon mixture into a greased 13"x9" baking pan; arrange unbaked biscuits on top. Bake, uncovered, at 375 degrees for 15 minutes, or until bubbly and biscuits are golden. Makes 8 servings.

To remove an onion smell from your hands, simply rub
your hands with a stainless steel spoon while holding
them under cold running water.

Parmesan Baked Pork Chops

Coleen Lambert
Luxemburg, WI

These luscious pork chops just melt in your mouth.

1 c. Italian-flavored dry bread
   crumbs
1 c. grated Parmesan cheese
1 t. garlic powder

1 t. pepper
1 T. olive oil
4 boneless pork chops,
   1/2-inch thick

Mix bread crumbs, Parmesan cheese and seasonings in a shallow dish. Brush olive oil over pork chops and press into crumb mixture, coating well on both sides. Arrange pork chops in a greased 13"x9" baking pan. Bake, uncovered, at 350 degrees for 40 to 45 minutes, until pork chops are tender and golden. Makes 4 servings.

A pat of herb butter is heavenly on warm rolls...try it on baked fish too. Blend together softened butter, chopped fresh chives or marjoram and a little lemon zest. Roll up in wax paper and chill, then slice to serve.

Ham Fried Rice

Angel Fridley
Staunton, VA

I learned this speedy recipe from a friend at work and it has become one of my oldest son Isaiah's favorite dishes. That's what makes it special to us! You can substitute cooked chicken or other veggies like sliced mushrooms and bean sprouts to make it your own too.

2 c. cooked ham, chopped
1 c. celery, chopped
1 c. onion, chopped
2 t. oil
2 c. cooked rice

1/4 c. soy sauce, or to taste
2 T. butter, sliced
3 eggs
pepper to taste

In a large skillet over medium heat, combine ham, celery, onion and oil. Sauté until onion is translucent. Add cooked rice and soy sauce; mix well. Make a well in the center; add butter. Break eggs into skillet over melted butter. Cook and scramble eggs until set, breaking up with spatula. Season with pepper. Mix eggs into ham mixture. Makes 8 servings.

At the end of the week, turn leftovers into a buffet-style meal. Set out casserole portions in pretty dishes, toss veggies into a salad and add a basket of warm rolls. Arrange everything on a counter...everyone is sure to come looking for their favorites!

Philly Cheesesteak Supreme Pizza

Megan Kreplin
Coxsackie, NY

We love pizza night in our house and a change from the usual is so much fun! The beef & veggie mixture marinades for a few hours, and it's easy to take a few minutes in the morning to get it ready and pop it in the fridge. Then it's pizza for dinner in no time.

1/4 c. olive oil
2 T. red wine vinegar
1-1/2 t. minced garlic
3/4 t. salt
pepper to taste
2 c. cooked deli roast beef,
   shredded

1/2 c. onion, thinly sliced
1 green pepper, thinly sliced
1 c. sliced mushrooms
1 ball store-bought pizza dough,
   room temperature
2 c. shredded mozzarella or
   provolone cheese

In a large plastic zipping bag, combine olive oil, vinegar, garlic, salt and pepper. Squeeze bag to combine ingredients. Add beef, onion, green pepper and mushrooms to bag; toss to coat. Seal bag; refrigerate for 4 to 24 hours. Drain marinade from beef and vegetables; discard marinade. Roll out pizza dough; place on an ungreased 15" round pizza stone or pizza pan. Arrange beef and vegetables over dough; top with cheese. Bake at 375 degrees for 20 to 25 minutes, until crust is golden and cheese is melted. Makes 8 servings.

A make-it-yourself pizza party is great for pizza-loving youngsters! Set out ready-to-bake pizza crusts and lots of toppings and let party guests be creative.

Crazy Crust Pizza

Vicki Meredith
Grandview, IN

This is crazy easy to make! If you're a pepperoni fan, just substitute a cup of pepperoni slices for the ground beef or sausage... no need to brown them.

1-1/2 lbs. ground beef or ground
    pork sausage
1 c. plus 1 t. all-purpose flour,
    divided
2 eggs, beaten
2/3 c. milk
1 t. dried oregano

1 t. salt
1/8 t. pepper
1/4 c. onion, chopped
4-oz. can mushroom pieces,
    drained
1 c. pizza sauce
1 c. shredded mozzarella cheese

In a skillet over medium heat, brown beef or sausage; drain and set aside. Lightly grease a 12" to 14" round pizza pan and dust with one teaspoon flour; set aside. In a small bowl, combine remaining flour, eggs, milk and seasonings; mix well until smooth. Pour batter into pan; tilt pan so batter covers bottom. Arrange meat, onion and mushrooms over batter. Place pan on low rack of oven. Bake at 425 degrees for 25 to 30 minutes, until crust is deeply golden. Remove from oven; drizzle with pizza sauce and sprinkle with cheese. Return to oven for 5 minutes, or until cheese is melted. Makes 10 to 12 servings.

Whip up some no-cooking-needed pizza sauce in a jiffy. In a blender, combine a can of seasoned diced tomatoes, a little garlic and a shake of Italian seasoning. Purée to the desired consistency.

Ashley's Turkey Burgers

Leona Krivda
Belle Vernon, PA

I got this recipe from my daughter-in-law Ashley. These burgers are really good, whether cooked on the stove or on the grill, and we make them quite often. Add your favorite burger toppings, if you like... we don't think they need anything else!

1/4 c. mayonnaise
1 T. Dijon mustard
1/4 c. pure maple syrup, divided
1-1/4 to 1-1/2 lbs. ground
   turkey
1/4 c. real bacon bits

1/2 c. chunky applesauce
1 t. poultry seasoning
1/2 t. salt
1/4 t. pepper
4 hamburger buns, split
   and toasted

In a small bowl, mix mayonnaise, mustard and 2 tablespoons maple syrup; set aside for sauce. In a large bowl, combine remaining maple syrup and other ingredients except buns. Mix well. With moistened hands, form into 4 patties. Grill or pan-fry patties over low heat to desired doneness, about 10 minutes per side. When done, brush patties with half of sauce. Brush toasted buns with remaining sauce; place patties on buns and serve. Makes 4 servings.

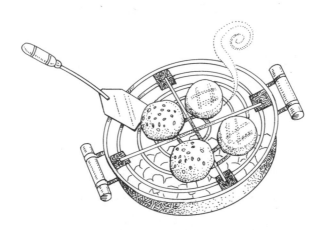

Burger buns just taste better toasted...and they won't get soggy! Butter buns lightly and place them on a hot grill for 30 seconds to one minute on each side, until toasty.

Bacon-Ranch Turkey Sloppy Joes

Rachel Kowasic
Valrico, FL

I was in the mood for a different type of Sloppy Joes and this recipe is what I came up with. The kids loved it!

2 green onions, chopped
1 clove garlic, minced
1 to 2 t. oil
1 lb. ground turkey

1/2 c. fresh baby spinach
1/2 c. ranch salad dressing
1/3 c. real bacon bits
4 to 6 hamburger buns, split

In a skillet over medium heat, sauté green onions and garlic in oil. Add turkey; cook and crumble until no longer pink. Drain; add spinach and cook until wilted. Add salad dressing and bacon bits; stir to combine and heat through. To serve, spoon onto buns. Makes 4 to 6 servings.

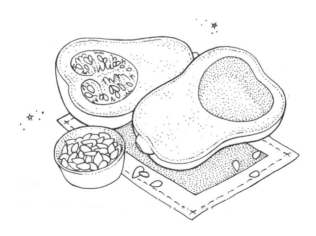

Serve up some tasty squash fries. Peel a butternut squash, slice into strips and place on a lightly greased baking sheet. Bake at 425 degrees for about 40 minutes, turning once, until tender. Season to taste and serve warm.

Judy's Sloppy Joes

Sue Klapper
Muskego, WI

For many years now I've hosted a post-Christmas party for my extended family. I provide this for our large group of sometimes 40 people. My cousin's husband, who's the cook in the family, was so impressed the first time I made it. "You made this from scratch!" he exclaimed. It is the perfect mix of sweet-and-sour and can be doubled or tripled as needed. Enjoy this for your next large group!

3 lbs. ground beef
2 onions, chopped
1 c. celery, sliced
1-1/2 c. catsup, or more to taste
2 T. brown sugar, packed, or
    more to taste

2 T. vinegar
1 T. Worcestershire sauce
Optional: 1 T. all-purpose flour
10 to 12 hamburger buns, split

In a skillet over medium heat, brown beef with onions and celery; drain. In a bowl, combine catsup, brown sugar, vinegar and Worcestershire sauce. Add to beef mixture; cook until simmering. Reduce heat to low; simmer for 10 to 15 minutes. If desired, stir in flour and simmer several more minutes, until thickened. To serve, spoon onto hamburger buns. Makes 10 to 12 servings.

Remember the vegetarians at your next cookout. Portabella mushrooms and thick slices of eggplant grill up into bun-filling treats. Pita rounds stuffed with grilled veggies are a delicious choice too.

Tavern Burgers

Amy Perling
Altoona, IA

This is a quick & easy lunch or supper that can be made ahead of time and reheated.

1 c. water
3/4 c. catsup
1 t. chili powder
1/2 t. Worcestershire sauce
2 lbs. lean ground beef

1 to 2 onions, chopped
2 T. mustard
salt and pepper to taste
8 hamburger buns, split
Optional: 8 cheese slices

Combine water, catsup, chili powder and Worcestershire sauce in a large deep skillet over medium heat. Bring to a boil; cook for 5 minutes, stirring often. Add beef, onions, mustard, salt and pepper. Cook until beef is thoroughly cooked and crumbled, about 30 minutes. To serve, spoon onto hamburger buns. Top each with a cheese slice, if desired. Makes 8 servings.

For a quick & tasty side, slice fresh tomatoes in half and sprinkle with minced garlic, Italian seasoning and grated Parmesan cheese. Broil until tomatoes are tender, about 5 minutes...scrumptious!

Sweetly Seasoned Hamburgers

Sarah Gardner
Schuylerville, NY

Whenever I make hamburgers, I double the recipe so I can freeze some for future dinners. My family loves these because they taste so good, you won't need to load on the fixings. They are good just they way they are. Enjoy your delicious burgers!

1/2 c. brown sugar, packed
2 t. paprika
1 t. salt
1 t. pepper
1/2 t. garlic powder
1/4 t. chili powder

2-1/2 lbs. lean ground beef
6 to 8 potato buns or other
    hamburger buns, split
Optional: favorite burger
    toppings

In a large bowl, mix brown sugar and seasonings. Add beef and mix well, using your hands. Form into 6 to 8 patties, about the size of the palm of your hand. Press a dimple into the center of each patty. Grill or pan-fry patties over low heat to desired doneness, 8 to 10 minutes per side. Serve burgers on buns with desired toppings. To freeze, place patties individually in plastic sandwich bags, place in a plastic freezer container and freeze; thaw before cooking. Makes 6 to 8 servings.

Make your own seasoning mixes! If you have a favorite busy-day recipe that calls for lots of different herbs or spices, measure them out into several small plastic zipping bags and label. Later, when time is short, just pull out a bag and add it to your recipe.

Snacks
for Parties & Everyday

Pizza Nachos

Mel Chencharick
Julian, PA

Nachos and pizza...they're a perfect combination! A great snack for after school, for watching the game or just for any occasion with friends.

12-oz. pkg. tortilla chips, divided
3 c. shredded pizza-blend cheese, divided
15-oz. can pizza sauce, divided

5-oz. pkg. pepperoni sticks, coarsely chopped and divided
Optional: sliced black or green olives, chopped green or red peppers

Divide tortilla chips between 2 large microwave-safe plates; arrange chips to cover plates. For each plate, top the chips with 1/2 cup cheese, half of sauce, another 1/2 cup cheese and half of pepperoni. Add olives and peppers, if using; top with remaining cheese. Microwave, uncovered, for 2 to 3 minutes, until cheese melts. Serve warm. Makes 4 to 6 servings.

When serving appetizers, a good rule of thumb for quantities is six to eight servings per person if dinner will follow, and 12 to 15 per person it it's an appetizer-only gathering. Enjoy!

Mini Deep-Dish Pizzas

Krista Marshall
Fort Wayne, IN

We love deep-dish pizza, but who has time to make it? These delicious bites make a fantastic appetizer, kids' party snack or even a light supper with a green salad on the side.

15-oz. can pizza sauce
1/2 c. grated Parmesan cheese
1 T. Italian seasoning
4 large flour tortillas

1 c. shredded mozzarella cheese
12 slices turkey pepperoni, quartered

In a small bowl, combine pizza sauce, Parmesan cheese and seasoning; stir well and set aside. Spray 12 muffin cups with non-stick vegetable spray. Using a glass tumbler or the empty, rinsed pizza sauce can, cut 3 rounds from each tortilla. Rounds should be just a little larger than muffin cups. Gently press tortilla rounds into muffin cups, covering each cup on the bottom and up the sides a little. Spoon 2 tablespoons sauce mixture into each cup; sprinkle with mozzarella cheese. Top each cup with 4 pieces pepperoni. Bake at 400 degrees for 10 to 15 minutes, until golden and crisp. Let stand 2 minutes; remove from muffin tin with a fork. Serve warm. Makes 6 servings of 2 mini pizzas each.

The simplest way to plan a party...choose a theme! Whether it's Fiesta Night, Fifties Diner or Oktoberfest, a theme suggests appropriate dishes, decorations and music, and gives guests something fun to look forward to.

Ham-It-Up Snacks

Tracy Stoll
Seville, OH

Guests will love these simple-to-make rolls. They're simple to make ahead...cover and refrigerate up to 2 hours before baking.

8-oz. tube refrigerated
   crescent rolls
4 thin slices cooked deli ham
4 t. mustard

1 c. shredded Swiss or Cheddar
   cheese
2 T. sesame seed

Unroll rolls; separate into 4 long rectangles. Press perforations to seal. Place one slice ham on each rectangle; spread ham with mustard and sprinkle with cheese. Starting on the shortest side, roll up each rectangle and press edges to seal. Coat rolls with sesame seeds. Cut each roll into 5 slices, making 20 in all. Place slices cut-side down on an ungreased baking sheet. Bake at 375 degrees for 15 to 20 minutes, until golden. Makes 20 snacks.

Serve up savory spreads with homemade toast dippers. Use cookie cutters to cut out fun shapes from slices of bread, then brush cut-outs with butter and a sprinkling of herbs. Bake in a 200-degree oven until crisp and golden.

Baked Broccoli & Bacon Bites

Cynthia Johnson
Verona, WI

These savory morsels are delicious all on their own...
even better with your favorite dipping sauce.

1 bunch broccoli flowerets
5 to 6 slices bacon
1/2 c. shredded mozzarella
   cheese

2 eggs, lightly beaten
1 c. dry bread crumbs
salt and pepper to taste

Steam or lightly cook broccoli; drain and chop. Meanwhile, cook bacon until crisp; drain and crumble. Transfer broccoli and bacon to a large bowl. Add remaining ingredients. Form mixture into balls the size of a golf ball. Place balls into greased muffin cups or on a greased baking sheet. Bake at 375 degrees for about 15 to 20 minutes, until golden. Makes 12 pieces.

Use tiered cake stands to serve bite-size appetizers...
so handy, and they take up less space on the buffet table
than setting out several serving platters.

Tuscan White Bean Dip

Jennifer Rose Blay
Puyallup, WA

When I got bored with hummus dip, I came up with this Italian version using cannellini beans. I hope you enjoy this as much as my husband and I do! For a different flavor, add 1/2 to one teaspoon of fresh rosemary or other chopped herbs. Buon appetito!

15-oz. can cannellini beans,
    drained and rinsed
1 clove garlic, minced
2 T. red onion, diced
1/3 c. fresh Italian parsley,
    shredded
3 T. shredded Parmesan and
    Romano cheese

2 T. lemon juice
3 T. extra virgin olive oil
1/8 t. cayenne pepper
salt and pepper to taste
pita chips, snack crackers or
    cut-up vegetables

In a food processor, combine beans, garlic, onion, parsley and cheese. Add lemon juice, olive oil and cayenne pepper. Process for one to 2 minutes, until smooth. Add salt and pepper. Dip may be covered and refrigerated up to 4 days. Serve with pita chips, snack crackers or vegetables. Makes 6 servings.

The secret to being a relaxed hostess...choose foods that can be prepared in advance. At party time, simply pull from the fridge and serve, or pop into a hot oven as needed.

Stephanie's Easy Salsa

Stephanie D'Esposito
Ravena, NY

I love this simple salsa recipe...I can make it anytime as I usually have most of the ingredients on hand. Adding just a few freshly chopped ingredients makes the salsa zesty and delicious.

3 10-cans diced tomatoes with green chiles
15-1/2 oz. can black beans, drained
11-oz. can sweet corn and diced peppers, drained
3 T. Italian salad dressing

1 c. fresh cilantro, chopped
1 red onion, chopped
1 jalapeño pepper, chopped
3 cloves garlic, minced
salt to taste
Optional: hot pepper sauce to taste

Drain 2 cans tomatoes; do not drain the remaining can. Combine tomatoes in a large bowl. Add remaining ingredients except salt and hot sauce; stir to mix. Season with salt and a few drops of hot sauce, if desired. Cover and refrigerate until serving time. Makes 14 servings.

When burgers, hot dogs, tacos or baked potatoes are on the menu, set up a topping bar with bowls of shredded cheese, catsup or salsa, crispy bacon and other tasty stuff. Everyone can just help themselves to their favorite toppings.

Laura's Awesome Onion & Cucumber Dip

Lisa Ann DiNunzio
Vineland, NJ

No gathering, special event or party would be complete without my sister's awesome dip. Diced cucumber adds such a refreshing touch... once people go in for a taste, it's all over! More often than not, she has to double the recipe.

1-1/2 c. sour cream or plain
   Greek yogurt
8-oz. pkg. cream cheese,
   softened
1/2 c. mayonnaise
3 T. pure maple syrup

1.35-oz. pkg. onion soup mix
1 large English cucumber, peeled
   and diced
sliced vegetables, crackers,
   pretzels or chips

In a large bowl, combine sour cream or yogurt, cream cheese, mayonnaise, maple syrup and soup mix. Beat with an electric mixer on medium speed until smooth; stir in cucumber. Cover and refrigerate at least 4 hours. Serve with a variety of fresh vegetables, crackers, pretzels or chips. Makes 12 to 16 servings.

Dip to go! Spoon some creamy vegetable dip into a tall plastic cup and add crunchy celery and carrot sticks, red pepper strips, cucumber slices and snow pea pods. Add a lid and the snack is ready to tote. Be sure to keep it chilled.

Parmesan Dill Dressing & Dip

Wendy Ball
Battle Creek, MI

I like to make our mealtimes special with lots of homemade items, both for everyday and for holidays. This salad dressing is easy to make and stores very well in the refrigerator. Enjoy it as a salad dressing or a dip for your favorite fresh veggies.

1-1/2 c. mayonnaise	2 T. whipping cream or milk
3/4 to 1 c. shredded Parmesan cheese	3 cloves garlic, chopped
	1 t. pepper
3 T. dill weed	1/2 t. onion powder

Blend all ingredients in a bowl. Cover and refrigerate until serving time. If serving as a vegetable dip, arrange assorted vegetables around bowl. If using as a salad dressing, thin to pouring consistency with a little more cream or milk, as needed. Makes about 2 cups.

Make an easy substitution...try using thick Greek yogurt instead of sour cream or mayonnaise. You'll get all the delicious richness, but with fewer calories.

Homemade Soft Pretzels

Vickie

*Making pretzels with your kids or grandkids is so much fun!
Then enjoy your creations for snacking or alongside a steamy
bowl of soup instead of a hot roll.*

1 env. active dry yeast	4 c. all-purpose flour
1-1/2 c. warm water	1 egg yolk
1 T. sugar	1 T. water
2 t. salt	1/4 c. coarse salt

In a large bowl, dissolve yeast in very warm water, 110 degrees. Add
sugar and salt; stir until dissolved. Add flour, one cup at a time; mix
well. Turn dough out onto a floured surface; knead for 5 minutes.
Divide dough into 2 parts; divide each half into 8 pieces. Roll into thin
ropes; shape into pretzel twists. Place pretzels on well-greased baking
sheets. Whisk together egg yolk and water in a cup; brush over tops
of pretzels and sprinkle with salt. Bake at 425 degrees for 15 to
20 minutes, until golden. Makes 16 pretzels.

Pick up a dozen pint–size Mason jars...perfect for serving
frosty beverages at casual get–togethers.

Warm Foccacia Dippers

Lori Ritchey
Denver, PA

So easy and delicious! Perfect with soup or pasta dishes.

16-oz. loaf foccacia bread
1-1/2 c. shredded mozzarella
   cheese

1 t. dried rosemary, crumbled
Garnish: warm spaghetti sauce

Heat broiler. Place foccacia on a baking sheet. Sprinkle with cheese and rosemary. Broil 3 minutes, or until cheese is nicely melted. Cut foccacia into 16 wedges. Serve warm with spaghetti sauce for dipping. Makes 16 wedges.

Crazy Kids Cheese Straws

Gladys Kielar
Whitehouse, OH

When kids help make the food, they're sure to eat it! You can find the frozen puff pastry in the freezer section of the grocery store.

1 sheet frozen puff pastry,
   about 14 by 12 inches
1 egg white

2 t. water
1-1/2 t. grated Parmesan cheese

Thaw puff pastry at room temperature for about 30 minutes; lay on a floured surface. In a small bowl, whisk together egg white and water. Brush egg mixture over pastry with a pastry brush; sprinkle with Parmesan cheese. With a pizza cutter or knife, cut pastry crosswise into 1/2-inch wide strips. Place strips on an ungreased baking sheet; gently twist several times. Bake at 400 degrees for 10 minutes, or until golden. Makes 15 to 20 straws.

For stand-up parties, make it easy on guests by serving foods that can be eaten in one or two bites.

Crispy Oven–Fried Chicken Wings

Jennie Gist
Gooseberry Patch

Who doesn't like a big platter of chicken wings? We love these crisp flavorful wings. They're baked instead of fried, so they're a little healthier.

1/2 to 3/4 c. butter, melted
1 c. seasoned panko bread
   crumbs
1 c. grated Parmesan cheese
1/8 t. garlic powder

1/8 t. onion powder
1/8 t. salt
1/8 t. pepper
4 lbs. chicken wings, cut
   into sections

Line a baking sheet with aluminum foil and spray with non-stick vegetable spray. Set a wire rack on baking sheet; set aside. Place melted butter in a shallow dish. In a separate shallow dish, combine bread crumbs, cheese and seasonings. Dip chicken wings into melted butter; press into crumb mixture to coat well. Arrange wings on wire rack. Bake at 400 degrees about 30 minutes, until golden. Turn wings over. Return to oven for 20 to 30 minutes, or until evenly golden and chicken juices run clear. Makes about 30 wings.

A tray of warm, moistened towels is a must when serving sticky barbecue ribs or chicken wings! Dampen fingertip towels in water and a dash of lemon juice, roll up and microwave on high for 10 to 15 seconds.

Snacks for Parties & Everyday

Feta & Veggie Stuffed Mushrooms

Jackie Smulski
Lyons, IL

Stuffed mushrooms are a must on any party tray! We like these because they're much lighter than usual.

1/2 c. herb-flavored stuffing mix
1/4 c. butter, softened
1/4 c. celery, finely minced
1/4 c. zucchini, minced
1/4 c. red or yellow pepper, minced

salt and pepper to taste
3/4 lb. baby portabella mushrooms or large white mushrooms, stems removed
2 T. crumbled feta cheese

In a bowl, combine stuffing, butter, celery, zucchini and red or yellow pepper. Season with salt and pepper. Spoon mixture evenly into mushroom caps. Place mushrooms on an ungreased baking sheet. Bake, uncovered, at 400 degrees for 20 minutes, until hot and bubbly. Mushrooms may also be placed in a grill pan and grilled over indirect heat, covered, for about 10 minutes. Remove from oven or grill; top with cheese. Serve warm. Makes 4 to 6 servings.

A quick and tasty appetizer in an instant...place a block of cream cheese on a serving plate, spoon sweet-hot pepper jelly over it and serve with crisp crackers. Tastes great with fruit chutney or spicy salsa too!

Cucumber Sliders

Wendy Ball
Battle Creek, MI

I used to make these tasty morsels as single snacks before I had an "Aha!" moment, why not make them sliders? Any leftover cream cheese is great stuffed in celery sticks, sprinkled with celery salt.

1 English cucumber, ends
   trimmed
8-oz. pkg. cream cheese,
   softened, or 6-oz. container
   onion & chive cream cheese

1 to 2 T. whipping cream or milk
16-oz. pkg. sliced party
   pumpernickel bread
celery salt to taste

With a fork or vegetable peeler, score cucumber lengthwise, making decorative stripes. Slice cucumber into 1/4-inch slices; set aside. With an electric mixer on medium speed, beat cream cheese, adding enough cream or milk for a spreadable consistency. To assemble, spread each bread slice with one to 1-1/2 teaspoons cream cheese. Top with a cucumber slice; sprinkle with celery salt and top with another bread slice. Makes 8 to 12 sliders.

Broiled Onion Toast

Irene Robinson
Cincinnati, OH

This warm, savory appetizer is very easy and very good. It may be assembled ahead of time, then broiled just before serving.

1 Bermuda onion, finely
   chopped
3 T. mayonnaise

salt and pepper to taste
8 slices French or rye bread

In a small bowl, combine onion, mayonnaise, salt and pepper. Spread mixture on bread. Place on a broiler pan. Broil until bubbly and golden, watching closely. Serve hot. Makes 8 servings.

May our house always be too small
to hold all of our friends.
– Myrtle Reed

Hot Pepperoni Dip

*Kathy Courington
Canton, GA*

*I sampled this dip at a holiday party and begged for the recipe.
It's so simple and good. You're sure to enjoy it too!*

8-oz. pkg. cream cheese,
  softened
15-oz. jar pizza sauce
1/3 c. onion, chopped
1-1/2 c. shredded pizza-blend
  cheese

6-oz. can sliced black olives,
  drained
3-1/2 oz. pkg. pepperoni, sliced
  or chopped
round buttery crackers or chips

Spread cream cheese in the bottom of an ungreased 2-quart casserole
dish. Layer with remaining ingredients except crackers or chips in
order given, ending with desired amount of pepperoni. Bake,
uncovered, at 350 degrees for 20 minutes, until hot and cheese is
melted. Serve with crackers or chips. Makes 8 to 12 servings.

Creamy hot dips are twice as tasty with homemade baguette
crisps. Thinly slice a French loaf on the diagonal and arrange
slices on a baking sheet. Sprinkle with olive oil and garlic
powder, then bake at 400 degrees for 12 to 15 minutes.

Bacon, Egg & Cheese Spread

Brenda Melancon
McComb, MS

I created this tasty recipe for my children and grandchildren when they come to visit, to tide them over while Maw Maw makes dinner. Adults love it on crackers, while children like it in sandwiches. If the kids are very young, you may want to use less hot sauce. The adults can add extra, if desired, as we Cajuns usually do.

16-oz. pkg. bacon, crisply
    cooked and crumbled
6 eggs, hard-boiled, peeled and
    finely chopped
1/2 c. shredded Cheddar cheese
1/2 c. sweet pickle relish
3 T. sweet onion, finely chopped
1/2 c. mayonnaise

1/3 c. sour cream
1 T. mustard
1-1/4 t. hot pepper sauce,
    or to taste
1 t. paprika
salt to taste
bread slices or crackers

In a large bowl, combine bacon, eggs, cheese, relish and onion; set aside. In a separate bowl, whisk together mayonnaise, sour cream, mustard and hot sauce. Add to bacon mixture; stir well. Sprinkle with paprika and salt; stir. Cover and chill for 2 hours. Serve as a spread on bread or crackers. Makes 3 cups.

Hard-boiled eggs made easy! Cover eggs with an inch of water in a saucepan and place over medium-high heat. As soon as the water boils, cover the pan and remove from heat. Let stand for 18 to 20 minutes...cover with ice water, peel and they're done.

Smoked Chicken Antipasto

*Courtney Stultz
Columbus, KS*

One year, I decided to toss together some holiday leftovers and this antipasto was created. It is delicious served with crackers or pita chips. You can even use a different meat as the main ingredient, such as roast turkey or beef.

1/4 c. cooked smoked chicken, diced
1/4 c. kalamata olives, sliced
1/4 c. artichokes, chopped
1/4 c. roasted red peppers, chopped

1 t. Italian salad dressing or red wine vinaigrette
Optional: 1/2 t. white wine
snack crackers or pita chips

In a small bowl, combine chicken, olives, artichokes and peppers. Drizzle with salad dressing and wine, if using; stir until combined. Cover and refrigerate at least 30 minutes before serving. Serve with crackers or pita chips. Makes 4 servings.

Set out bowls of unshelled nuts for a quick appetizer that will keep early-arriving guests busy while you put the finishing touches on the party table. Don't forget the nutcracker!

Ranchero Sauce & Dip

Kathleen McKenney
Quebec, Canada

This sauce is wonderful on barbecued ribs and chicken. I even serve it as a dip with nachos. If fresh tomatoes are out of season, you can use canned diced tomatoes, well drained.

1/2 T. olive oil
1/3 c. onion, chopped
1/2 t. garlic, minced
1-1/2 c. tomatoes, chopped
1/2 jalapeño pepper, finely
    chopped

1 t. tomato paste
1/2 t. brown sugar, packed
1/2 t. fresh oregano, minced
1/2 t. salt
1/2 t. lime juice

Heat oil in saucepan over medium heat. Add onion and garlic; sauté until soft. Add remaining ingredients to pan. Increase heat to medium-high and bring to a boil. Reduce heat to low and simmer for 10 minutes, stirring occasionally. Remove from heat and let cool. Keep refrigerated. Makes 4 servings.

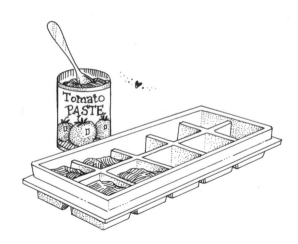

If a recipe calls for just a partial can of tomato paste, freeze the rest in ice cube trays, then pop out and store in a freezer bag. Frozen cubes can be dropped into simmering soups or sauces for added flavor...easy!

Sherri's Happy Sauce

Stefani Keeton
Cement, OK

My friend Sherri makes this all the time...her two older kids love it! When they know she's making it, they won't stay out of the kitchen until it's done!

8-oz. container sour cream
6 sprigs fresh cilantro with
  stems
1-oz. pkg. ranch salad dressing
  mix

10 slices pickled jalapeño
  peppers
chips or cut-up vegetables

To a food processor, add sour cream, cilantro, dressing mix and jalapeño peppers. Process until smooth; transfer to a serving bowl. Cover and chill for one hour. Serve with chips or vegetables. Makes 10 servings.

Creamy Honey–Mustard Spread

Kathie Craig
Burlington, WI

I enjoy shopping at farmers' markets for local produce and honey. This recipe is a summer staple at our house and can be used as a spread or dip. We like it on sandwiches, burgers and brats...even add it to potato salad!

8-oz. jar Dijon mustard
1/3 c. honey

1 T. brown sugar, packed

In a small bowl, mix mustard, honey and brown sugar until well blended and brown sugar is dissolved. Spoon into a jar with a lid; cover. May be refrigerated up to 6 months. Makes about one cup.

Create a warm party glow in a jiffy, using box graters picked up at flea markets. Simply tuck a votive or tealight inside...so simple!

Mini Vegetable Pizza Cups

Tena Huckleby
Morristown, TN

These tasty snacks are my own creation. Made with a tube of crescent rolls and a little of this & that from the pantry, they're perfect for snack, lunch or brunch.

8-oz. tube refrigerated
   crescent rolls
1/2 c. pizza sauce
1 T. fresh oregano, chopped
2 t. salt
1 t. pepper

1/4 c. grated Parmesan cheese
1 t. garlic powder
2 T. tomato, diced
2 T. onion, chopped
2 T. broccoli, chopped
1/2 c. shredded Cheddar cheese

Spray 8 muffin cups with non-stick vegetable spray. Separate crescent rolls; press one roll into each muffin cup. Fill each cup 1/2 full of pizza sauce. In a bowl, mix together remaining ingredients except Cheddar cheese. Evenly spoon mixture into each cup. Spread Cheddar cheese over top. Bake at 350 degrees for 12 to 15 minutes. Cool slightly; serve warm. Makes 8 pieces.

Guests are sure to appreciate pitchers of ice water they can help themselves to. Make some fancy party ice cubes by tucking sprigs of mint into ice cube trays before freezing.

Easy Cheese Puffs

Leona Krivda
Belle Vernon, PA

This is a recipe you can tuck in the freezer to bake when someone comes to visit. I love having things like this on hand! My grandkids are always looking in the freezer to see what they can find.

16-oz. loaf French bread, crusts
   trimmed
1 c. shredded sharp Cheddar
   cheese

3-oz. pkg. cream cheese,
   softened
1/2 c. margarine
2 egg whites

Cut bread into 2-inch cubes and place in a large bowl; set aside. In a saucepan over low heat, melt cheeses with margarine, stirring occasionally. Remove from heat. In a large bowl, with an electric mixer on high speed, beat egg whites until stiff peaks form. Fold 1/4 of egg whites into cheese mixture; fold cheese mixture into remaining egg whites. Spoon cheese mixture over bread cubes; toss to coat each cube very well. Place cubes in a single layer on an ungreased baking sheet. Bake at 400 degrees for 12 minutes, or until bubbly and golden. To make ahead, place puffs on baking sheet, but do not bake. Place in freezer. When cheese puffs are frozen, transfer them to a plastic freezer bag and return to freezer. When ready to serve, put frozen puffs on baking sheet; bake as directed above. Makes 10 to 12 servings.

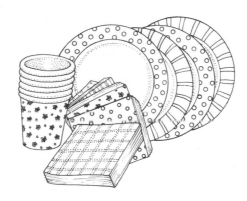

Festive trimmings can turn the simplest fare into a feast.
Pick up some brightly colored napkins and table coverings at
the nearest dollar store and you're halfway to a party!

Smoked Gouda Pimento Cheese

*Andrea Heyart
Savannah, TX*

*Serve this cheesy blend as a dip with crackers, chips and
fresh veggies, or as a sandwich spread. However you serve it,
this updated classic makes fabulous finger food!*

1 c. smoked Gouda cheese,
   grated
1 c. shredded Cheddar cheese
8-oz. pkg. cream cheese,
   softened
1/2 c. mayonnaise

1/4 c. red onion, diced
1 green onion, diced
2-oz. jar chopped pimentos,
   drained
1/8 t. cayenne pepper

Combine all ingredients in a bowl; stir together until well blended.
Cover and chill for one hour before serving. Makes 2 cups.

The next time a party guest asks, "How can I help?"
be ready with an answer! Whether it's picking up a bag of ice,
setting the table or even bringing a special dessert, friends
are usually happy to lend a hand.

Curry Chicken Party Rolls

Paulette Alexander
Newfoundland, Canada

I love being able to make this tasty appetizer with ingredients I already have on hand. It makes a lot of servings and takes no time at all! You can even use raisins or apples instead of grapes, or green onion instead of celery. Add a few nuts if you like too.

1 boneless, skinless chicken
    breast, cooked and shredded
3 to 4 T. mayonnaise
2 to 3 T. grapes, thinly sliced

2 T. celery, finely diced
curry powder to taste
3 soft wraps

In a bowl, mix chicken with just enough mayonnaise to hold together. Add grapes, celery and curry powder. Spread mixture on wraps and roll up; cut into one-inch lengths. Serve immediately, or cover and refrigerate until serving time. Makes 8 to 10 servings.

fresh veggie Dip

Table tents are so handy! Fold a file card in half and jot down or rubber stamp the recipe name on one side. Set a table tent next to each dish so everyone will know just what's being served up.

Roasted Sesame & Honey Trail Mix

Lori Rosenberg
University Heights, OH

This is a great snack to take along on day hikes. The sweet & salty combo is always a hit, even with the family dog!

3 c. bite-size crispy cereal
   squares, any variety
3 c. waffle pretzels
3 c. sesame sticks
1 c. mixed nuts

3 T. butter, melted
1/4 c. honey
2 T. sesame seed, toasted
   if desired

In a large microwave-safe bowl, mix cereal, pretzels, sesame sticks and nuts; set aside. In a 2-cup microwave-safe measuring cup, microwave butter on high about 30 seconds, until melted. Stir in honey and sesame seed. Pour butter mixture over cereal mixture; stir until evenly coated. Microwave, uncovered, on high for 5 to 6 minutes, stirring every 2 minutes, until mixture just begins to turn golden. Spread on wax paper to cool. Store in an airtight container. Makes 20 servings of 1/2 cup each.

Nuts are yummy in crunchy snack mixes, but if you need to avoid them, try substituting dried fruit bits or sunflower kernels. Or just omit the nuts...your snack mix will still be tasty!

Lemon Pepper Popcorn

*Kim Hinshaw
Cedar Park, TX*

*This quick & tasty snack is healthier than prepackaged
microwave popcorn...so easy to do, too!*

1 T. coconut oil
2 t. lemon pepper seasoning

1/3 c. popcorn kernels
salt to taste

Place coconut oil, seasoning and 3 popcorn kernels in a heavy
saucepan. Cover and shake pan over medium heat until popcorn
kernels pop. Add remaining kernels to pan. Cover and continue
cooking while shaking pan over heat until all popping stops. Sprinkle
with salt and additional seasoning, if desired. Makes one serving of
2 cups.

Here's a quick trick if you're serving up popcorn to
a crowd. Use coffee filters as disposable bowls.
Afterwards, just toss 'em away!

Yummy Cannoli Dip

Kelly Ross
Coventry, CT

Cannolis have been our traditional (and favorite!) Christmas dessert for many generations. But I could never seem to make those shells just right. This sweet dip has all the taste of tradition without the hassle...just measure, stir and enjoy!

15-oz. container whole-milk
    ricotta cheese
1/3 c. powdered sugar
1/4 c. plain Greek yogurt or
    sour cream

1 t. vanilla extract
2/3 c. mini chocolate chips,
    divided
waffle cookies, strawberries

In a serving bowl, beat together cheese, powdered sugar, yogurt or sour cream and vanilla. Fold in 1/3 cup chocolate chips. Garnish with remaining chocolate chips. Serve immediately, or cover and chill. Serve with cookies and strawberries. Makes 2-1/2 cups.

Just One More Bite Fruit Dip

Marilyn Morel
Keene, NH

My sister Beth gave this recipe to me and it's sooo good, you just have to have one more bite! Easy to make, portable, budget-friendly and simply delicious. There's never any left over!

8-oz. container sour cream
1/4 c. light brown sugar, packed
1 T. vanilla extract

strawberries, pineapple chunks,
    apple wedges

In a serving bowl, mix sour cream, brown sugar and vanilla well. Cover and refrigerate until ready to serve. Serve with assorted fruit pieces. Makes 12 servings.

No-Bake Good Stuff

Betty Lou Wright
Hendersonville, TN

Such a scrumptious recipe, and so nutritious! It's fun to use a mix of white and milk chocolate chips. Doubling the recipe to fill a 13"x9" baking pan is a good idea...it gets gobbled up pretty quickly!

1 c. old-fashioned oats, uncooked
1/2 to 3/4 c. sweetened flaked coconut
1/2 to 3/4 c. raisins or sweetened dried cranberries
1/2 c. ground flax seed
1/2 c. natural creamy peanut butter
1/3 c. honey
1 t. vanilla extract
1/8 to 1/4 t. cinnamon
Optional: 1/2 c. semi-sweet chocolate chips

Mix all ingredients in a large bowl until well combined. Add a little more honey, if needed, to make mixture hold together. Press mixture into an 8"x8" baking pan lightly coated with non-stick vegetable spray. Cover and refrigerate for about one hour. Slice into squares or roll into balls. May keep refrigerated in an airtight container for up to a week. Makes 16 servings.

When shopping for cloth napkins, be sure to pick up an extra one! Use it to wrap around a flower pot, pitcher or pail and you'll always have a matching centerpiece.

Lee's Cheesy Apple Quesadillas

Leona Krivda
Belle Vernon, PA

When I get hungry and want just a little something, I like to make these quesadillas. They are easy, healthy and I always have the ingredients on hand. I usually eat half of one and share the other half with whoever else is home.

2 8-inch flour tortillas
1 Granny Smith apple, cored and
    thinly sliced

1/4 c. shredded Cheddar cheese

Place one tortilla on a griddle over medium-low heat. Cover tortilla with apple slices to within 1/2-inch of the edge. Sprinkle cheese over apple slices to cover well; top with remaining tortilla. As quesadilla cooks, press lightly around the edges with a spatula. Cook until golden on the bottom; turn and cook other side. Slide quesadilla onto a plate. Cut into 8 thin wedges with a pizza cutter; serve warm. Makes 2 servings, 4 wedges each.

Make your own baked tortilla chips. Spritz both sides of corn or flour tortillas with non–stick vegetable spray and cut into wedges. Microwave on high setting for 5 to 6 minutes, turning wedges over every 1-1/2 minutes. Sprinkle warm chips with sea salt and serve.

Cookies, Cakes & Pies...
Yum!

Toffee Bars

Cheryl Gerren
Port Saint Lucie, FL

*This simple recipe is delicious! It's a sweet treat
that is perfect for get-togethers.*

1 c. butter, softened
1 c. brown sugar, packed
1 t. vanilla extract
2 c. all-purpose flour

6-oz. pkg semi-sweet chocolate
  chips
1 c. chopped pecans

In a large bowl, blend together butter and brown sugar. Stir in vanilla.
Add flour and mix well. Stir in chocolate chips and pecans. Pat dough
into an ungreased 15"x10" jelly-roll pan. Bake at 350 degrees for 15 to
18 minutes. Cut into bars while still warm. Makes 15 to 18 bars.

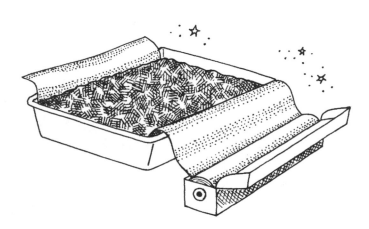

Make perfect bar cookies. Lay a length of aluminum foil
across the baking pan, extending a few inches on each side.
Grease, fill and bake as directed. After cooling, use the extra
foil as handles to lift out the cookies onto a cutting board.
Cut neatly into squares.

Chip-A-Roons

Susan Whitson
Telford, TN

Placed on a pretty dish, these macaroon cookies look great and taste even better!

16-oz. pkg. sweetened flaked coconut
14-oz. can sweetened condensed milk

3/4 c. semi-sweet chocolate chips
1/4 c. all-purpose flour
2 t. vanilla extract

Combine all ingredients in a large bowl; mix well. Drop batter onto greased baking sheets by teaspoonfuls. Bake at 350 degrees for 10 to 12 minutes, until golden. Using a spatula dipped in water, immediately remove cookies to a wire rack. Cool. Makes 3 dozen cookies.

Preheating the oven ensures evenly baked cookies. Turn on the oven and set it to the right temperature before starting to mix your cookie dough. The temperature will be just right when the cookies are ready to bake.

Special Snickerdoodles

Teresa Eller
Tonganoxie, KS

*These old-fashioned cookies are so good! Kids will giggle
when you tell them the name of the cookies.*

2 t. cinnamon
1-3/4 c. sugar, divided
1 c. shortening
2 eggs
1 t. almond extract

2-3/4 c. all-purpose flour
2 t. cream of tartar
1 t. baking soda
1/4 t. salt

In a small bowl, combine cinnamon and 1/4 cup sugar; set aside. In
a large bowl, with an electric mixer on low speed, beat together
remaining sugar, shortening, eggs and almond extract. Add remaining
ingredients; beat until smooth. Form dough into one-inch balls and roll
in cinnamon-sugar. Place balls on ungreased baking sheets. Bake at
400 degrees for about 10 minutes. Makes 1-1/2 dozen cookies.

Enjoy fresh-baked cookies in minutes by freezing some of
your cookie dough! Simply drop rounded spoonfuls on a
parchment-lined baking sheet, freeze until firm and transfer
to a plastic zipping bag. When you're ready to bake, just add
a few extra minutes of baking time.

Secret Kiss Snowballs

Sue Klapper
Muskego, WI

I got this recipe from a friend many years ago and have made it each Christmas since then. I don't know what I love best...the chocolate surprise inside each cookie, or the delicious pecan cookie itself. I pack these cookies in small tins for special friends and hostess gifts.

1 c. butter, softened
1/2 c. sugar
1 t. vanilla extract
2 c. all-purpose flour

1 c. pecans, finely chopped
36 milk chocolate drops,
   unwrapped
1 c. powdered sugar

Combine butter, sugar and vanilla in a large bowl. Beat with an electric mixer on medium speed until blended. Gradually add flour and nuts; beat on low speed until well blended. Cover and chill dough about one hour, until firm enough to handle. Shape one tablespoon dough around each chocolate drop and roll to form a ball, covering chocolate completely. Place balls on ungreased baking sheets. Bake at 375 degrees for 12 minutes, or until cookies are set but not browned. Cool slightly; roll in powdered sugar. Makes 3 to 4 dozen cookies.

A balanced diet is a cookie in each hand.
– Barbara Johnson

Mom's Sugar Cookies

Lynnette Jones
East Flat Rock, NC

My mom used to make these cookies for us all the time. They are so quick, easy and delicious. Be sure to use self-rising flour! For the 1/4 cup of sugar you can use colored sugar, if you like.

1 c. canola oil, divided
1 c. sugar, divided
2 eggs

2 t. vanilla extract
2 c. self-rising flour

Place 1/3 cup oil and 1/4 cup sugar in 2 separate small bowls; set aside. In a separate large bowl, beat eggs with a fork. Stir in vanilla and remaining oil; mix well. Stir in flour and remaining sugar. Drop dough by teaspoonfuls onto parchment paper-lined baking sheets. For each cookie, dip the bottom of a beverage glass into reserved oil, then into reserved sugar; gently press cookie with glass. Bake at 400 degrees for 8 to 10 minutes, until lightly golden. Remove to a wire rack; cool. Makes 3 dozen cookies.

Make your own colored sugar. Place 1/2 cup sugar in a plastic zipping bag, then add 5 to 6 drops of food coloring. Knead the bag until color is mixed throughout, then spread sugar on a baking sheet to dry.

Raisin Griddle Cake Cookies

Jessica Shrout
Flintstone, MD

*My dad loves raisin-filled cookies and these are the next best thing!
So easy, I used to make them as a little girl because they are so
easy...just mix, roll, cut and cook on a griddle. So fast when company
is coming. These cookies store well, but they won't last long!*

1-1/4 c. raisins	1 t. salt
2 c. hot water	1 t. nutmeg
3-1/2 c. all-purpose flour	1 c. butter-flavored shortening
1 c. sugar	1 egg, beaten
1-1/2 t. baking powder	1/2 c. milk
1/2 t. baking soda	oil for griddle

Combine raisins and hot water in a bowl; set aside. In a large bowl,
mix flour, sugar, baking powder, baking soda, salt and nutmeg. Cut in
shortening with 2 knives until crumbly. In a small bowl, whisk
together egg and milk; add to dough. Drain raisins and add to dough.
Stir to form a slightly stiff but smooth dough. Roll out dough on a
floured surface to 1/4-inch thick. Cut out dough with a round biscuit
cutter. Heat a griddle over medium heat until a drop of water dances
on the griddle. Oil griddle lightly. Add cookies, several at a time. Cook
for several minutes, until lightly golden on bottom; turn and cook
other side. Cool cookies on a wire rack. Dough may also be rolled into
a log shape, wrapped in wax paper or plastic wrap and frozen. Thaw,
slice and bake as needed. Makes about one dozen large cookies or
2 dozen small cookies.

Sprinkle powdered sugar on the work surface when
rolling out cookie dough...so much tastier than using flour
and it works just as well!

Zucchini Brownies

Lisa Sett
Thousand Oaks, CA

These rich chocolate brownies have two kinds of chocolate. They also have lots of grated zucchini, plus applesauce to replace some of the oil. So, they're healthier than usual...don't tell the kids!

2 c. all-purpose flour
1-1/4 c. sugar
1/2 c. baking cocoa
1-1/2 t. baking soda
1 t. salt
1/4 c. oil

1/4 c. unsweetened applesauce
1 egg, beaten
1 T. vanilla extract
2 c. zucchini, grated and drained
1 c. semi-sweet chocolate chips
Optional: powdered sugar

In a bowl, combine flour, sugar, cocoa, baking soda and salt; mix well. In a separate large bowl, mix together oil, applesauce, egg and vanilla. Add flour mixture to oil mixture; stir until well mixed. Batter will be thick. Fold in zucchini and chocolate chips. Spray a 13"x9" baking pan with non-stick vegetable spray; dust with cocoa. Spread batter in pan. Bake at 350 degrees for 20 to 25 minutes. Cut into squares; serve plain or dust with powdered sugar. Makes 12 to 15 brownies.

For perfectly cut brownies, refrigerate them in the pan
for about an hour after baking. Cut them with a plastic
knife for a clean cut every time!

Ruby's Whole-Wheat Honey & Molasses Cookies

Ruby Pruitt
Nashville, IN

While going through chemo for the third time, I decided I needed to eat healthier than ever before, so when I came across this recipe I tweaked it. It's well worth the time to make and the cookies are great. My husband is a meat & potatoes person and he said these were very good. That in itself is a compliment.

2-1/3 c. white whole-wheat flour
1 t. baking powder
1 t. baking soda
1/2 t. sea salt
2-1/2 t. ground ginger
1-1/2 t. ground cardamon

1 t. cinnamon
1/2 c. olive oil
2/3 c. molasses
1/4 c. honey
1 t. vanilla extract

In a food processor, combine flour, baking powder, baking soda, salt and spices. Blend well; set aside. Add oil to a small saucepan over low heat; heat just until warmed. Remove from heat. Add remaining ingredients to oil and stir well; transfer to a large bowl. Slowly add flour mixture to oil mixture; stir until well blended. Cover and refrigerate for 30 minutes. Form dough into balls, about 1-1/4 inches in diameter. Place balls on greased baking sheets. Flatten balls with a fork in a crisscross pattern. Bake at 350 degrees for 9 to 11 minutes, until set. Remove cookies to a wire rack to cool. Makes 2 dozen cookies.

Toss a few slices of apple in the cookie jar
to keep cookies soft and fresh.

191

Frosted Butter Meltaways

Mel Chencharick
Julian, PA

When I think back to the hundreds and hundreds of cookies I've made, this simple recipe has to be one of the easiest. It makes a lot, and with a drop or two of food coloring you can make these for any holiday or school color occasion, even weddings!

1-1/4 c. all-purpose flour
1 c. butter, softened

3/4 c. cornstarch
1/3 c. powdered sugar

Combine all ingredients in a large bowl. Beat with an electric mixer on medium speed, until fluffy. Divide dough into 4 equal parts and roll each into a smooth log. Wrap each log in floured wax paper. Chill dough at least 6 hours. At baking time, allow dough to stand at room temperature for 15 minutes to soften. Slice dough 1/4-inch thick and place on greased baking sheets. Bake at 350 degrees for 10 minutes, until golden. Cool cookies on wire racks. Pipe or dollop a small amount of Frosting onto cookies. Makes 8 dozen cookies.

Frosting:

1 c. powdered sugar
3-oz. pkg. cream cheese,
    softened

1/2 t. vanilla extract
1 to 2 drops food coloring

In a bowl, combine powdered sugar, cream cheese and vanilla. Beat with an electric mixer on medium speed until smooth and creamy. Beat in food coloring one drop at a time, to desired tint.

To soften butter quickly for a recipe, grate chilled sticks with a cheese grater.

Russian Tea Cookies

Lilia Keune
Biloxi, MS

This is an amazing cookie that melts in your mouth. The recipe was given to me by my friend's grandma. It's my go-to recipe when I need something really delicious.

1-1/2 c. butter, softened
1 t. salt
3/4 c. powdered sugar
1 T. vanilla extract

3 c. all-purpose flour
2 c. mini semi-sweet chocolate
   chips
1/2 c. pecans, finely chopped

In a large bowl, beat together butter, salt, powdered sugar and vanilla. Gradually add flour and mix well. Stir in chocolate chips and pecans. Shape tablespoonfuls of dough into one-inch logs. Place on ungreased baking sheets. Bake at 375 degrees for 12 minutes, or until lightly golden. Sift powdered sugar over hot cookies on baking sheets. Let stand for 10 minutes; remove cookies to wire racks. When cool, immediately store in an airtight container. Makes 4 dozen cookies.

Share homemade cookies with a friend. Wrap cookies
in a tea towel and tuck them into a basket along with
some packets of spiced tea. A sweet gift that says
"I'm thinking of you!"

Egg-Free Cocoa Cake

Carol Hummel
Kirkland, WA

*My dad requested this egg-free cake for his birthday for
literally decades! It is moist, yummy and great for
people who must avoid eggs for any reason.*

3 c. all-purpose flour
2 c. sugar
2 T. baking cocoa
2 t. baking soda
1 t. salt

2 c. warm water
3/4 c. oil
2 T. white vinegar
2 t. vanilla extract

Mix flour, sugar, cocoa, baking soda and salt in a large bowl. Add
remaining ingredients and mix thoroughly. Pour batter into a greased
and floured 13"x9" baking pan. Bake at 350 degrees for 30 minutes, or
until a wooden toothpick tests clean. For cupcakes, spoon batter into
24 greased muffin cups, filling 2/3 full. Bake at 350 degrees for 18 to
20 minutes. Makes 24 servings.

Create a charming cake stand with thrift-store finds. Attach a
glass plate with epoxy glue to a short glass vase or candle stand
for a base. Let dry completely before using...so clever!

Honey-Walnut Cake

Janet Sharp
Milford, OH

I bake this delicious cake after I have brought back fresh honey from the honey farm. I serve it with fresh fruit for breakfast or dessert.

2-1/2 c. all-purpose flour
1 t. baking powder
1-1/2 t. baking soda
1/2 t. salt
3/4 c. butter, softened
1/2 c. sugar

2 eggs
3/4 c. honey
1 t. vanilla extract
1 c. buttermilk
1/2 c. walnut pieces

In a bowl, combine flour, baking powder, baking soda, and salt. Mix well; set aside. In a large bowl, blend butter and sugar until fluffy. Add eggs, one at a time, and beat well. Stir in honey and vanilla. Add flour mixture to butter mixture alternately with buttermilk; stir well. Pour batter into a 9" round cake pan coated with non-stick vegetable spray; spread walnuts over batter. Bake at 350 degrees for 45 minutes, or until a wooden toothpick inserted in center of cake comes out clean. Turn out cake onto a wire rack; cool before slicing. Makes 8 servings.

No buttermilk? Stir one tablespoon vinegar or lemon juice into one cup milk and let stand 5 minutes before adding to a recipe.

Swedish Orange Cake

Delane Thorwart
Saint Marys, PA

A local bank was having a bake sale and this cake just stole my heart. When I cut the cake and tasted it, wow! I must have this recipe! To my surprise, a friend at the bank had made the cake and she shared the recipe with me. She said it was from an old Swedish cookbook.

1/2 c. butter, softened
1 c. sugar
2 eggs, separated
1 t. vanilla extract
1/2 c. walnuts, finely chopped

2 c. all-purpose flour
1/2 t. baking powder
1 t. baking soda
3/4 c. buttermilk

In a large bowl, beat butter until softened. Add sugar and blend until light and fluffy. Beat in egg yolks, one at a time; beat well after each addition. Add vanilla and walnuts. In a separate bowl, mix flour, baking powder and baking soda. Fold flour mixture into butter mixture alternately with buttermilk; set aside. With an electric mixer on high speed, beat egg whites until stiff peaks form. Fold egg whites into batter. Pour batter into a greased and floured 8" tube pan. Bake at 350 degrees for 50 to 60 minutes. For a 10" tube pan, reduce baking time to 40 minutes. Cool cake slightly; turn out of pan onto a cake plate. Drizzle Glaze over cake. Makes 10 servings.

Glaze:

zest and juice of 1 navel orange   1/2 c. sugar

Combine all ingredients; stir until sugar dissolves. Let stand while preparing cake.

For orange zest in a jiffy, use a vegetable peeler to remove very thin slices of the outer layer of peel. Mince finely with a paring knife.

Pineapple Sheet Cake

Marian Forck
Chamois, MO

This is a very good cake...you can hardly stop with one piece! I received this recipe from a co-worker and have made it many times.

2 eggs, beaten
2 c. sugar
20-oz. can crushed pineapple
2 c. all-purpose flour

1/2 t. baking powder
2 t. baking soda
1/8 t. salt
1 c. chopped pecans

In a large bowl, combine eggs, sugar and pineapple with juice. Mix well. Add remaining ingredients except pecans; mix well. Spread batter in a 15"x10" jelly-roll pan sprayed with non-stick vegetable spray. Bake at 350 degrees for 30 minutes. Spread cooled cake with Frosting; top with pecans. Cut into squares. Makes 12 to 15 servings.

Frosting:

8-oz. pkg. cream cheese, softened
1 t. vanilla extract

1/4 c. butter, melted and slightly cooled
2 c. powdered sugar

Combine all ingredients in a large bowl. Beat with an electric mixer on medium speed until smooth.

Offer mini portions of rich cobblers, cakes or pies in small cups. Guests can take "just a taste" of something sweet after a big dinner or sample several yummy treats.

Homemade Yellow Cake Mix

Audra Vanhorn-Sorey
Columbia, NC

*I love making my own cake mixes instead of buying them.
The difference in taste is unbelievable!*

1-1/2 c. all-purpose flour
1-1/2 c. cake flour
2 c. sugar
1/2 c. non-fat dry milk powder

1 T. baking powder
1 t. salt
1 c. butter, diced
1 T. vanilla extract

Add all ingredients except butter and vanilla to a food processor.
Process for 15 seconds, until combined. Add butter; lightly fluff with a
fork to coat with flour mixture. Add vanilla; pulse until mixture is
crumbly and fine. Immediately use in any recipe calling for a 2-layer
yellow cake mix, or freeze in a plastic zipping bag up to 2 months.
Makes 12 servings.

Cherry–Pineapple Dump Cake

Shirley Condy
Plainview, NY

*This cake is so good and nothing could be easier...try it with
blueberry pie filling too. Great for last-minute company!*

21-oz. can cherry pie filling
22-oz. can crushed pineapple,
   drained

18-1/2 oz. pkg. yellow cake mix
1 c. butter, diced

Spread pie filling in a lightly greased 13"x9" baking pan. Spread
pineapple over pie filling. Sprinkle dry cake mix over fruit. Do not add
anything to cake mix; do not mix layers. Scatter butter over top,
covering as much as possible. Bake at 350 degrees for one hour. Serve
warm. Makes 10 to 12 servings.

When draining canned fruit, freeze the juice in ice cube trays...
handy for adding a little sweetness to marinades and dressings.

Spicy Apple Dump Cake

Jill Steeley
Broken Arrow, OK

The delicious smell and taste of the spice and the surprising apple pie-like bottom layer makes this a great dessert for fall and winter. It's even tastier served warm with a scoop of ice cream.

4 to 5 Fuji or Gala apples, peeled, cored and thinly sliced
1-1/4 c. apple juice, divided
18-1/4 oz. pkg. spice cake mix
1/2 c. butter, melted
1/4 c. brown sugar, packed
1/4 c. rolled oats, uncooked
1/4 c. pecans, coarsely chopped

Arrange apple slices in the bottom of a lightly greased 13"x9" baking pan. Pour 1/2 cup apple juice over apples. Sprinkle dry cake mix over apples and smooth it evenly across the pan. Sprinkle remaining apple juice evenly across cake mix layer; drizzle with butter. For topping, mix brown sugar, oats, and pecans with a fork until no lumps remain. Sprinkle evenly over top. Bake at 350 degrees for about 40 minutes, until cake begins to turn golden. Makes 8 servings.

Scoops of ice cream are a perfect garnish for warm pies and puddings. Serve them in a snap...simply scoop ahead of time into paper muffin cup liners and freeze on a baking sheet.

That Crazy Tomato Cake

Shannon Hildebrandt
Saskatchewan, Canada

My friend Melanie introduced me to a similar recipe for using up the abundance of green tomatoes left over at summer's end. This recipe is quick to whip up and tastes delicious!

1/2 c. butter
1 c. brown sugar, packed
1/2 c. sugar
2 eggs, beaten
1/2 t. vanilla extract
2 c. all-purpose flour
1 t. baking soda

1/2 t. salt
1/2 t. pumpkin pie spice
1/8 t. ground ginger
3-1/2 c. green tomatoes, very
  finely diced
1/2 c. chopped pecans
Garnish: favorite white frosting

In a large bowl, blend butter and sugars. Add eggs and vanilla; beat until smooth and set aside. In a separate bowl, combine flour, baking soda, salt and spices. Add flour mixture to butter mixture, stirring until combined and thick. Add tomatoes; stir well until combined and batter starts to thin a bit. Stir in pecans. Pour batter into a greased 13"x9" baking pan. Bake at 350 degrees for 30 to 40 minutes, until a wooden toothpick tests clean when inserted in center of cake. Let cool before frosting. Makes 16 to 20 servings.

For guaranteed crumb-free frosting, add a very thin layer of frosting to a cake and refrigerate. When the frosting is firm, go ahead, frost and decorate as desired...it'll be beautiful!

Easy-Peasy Berry Cake

Peter Kay
Naples, FL

This is the easiest berry cake you can make. It's a great spur-of-the-moment dessert and it looks so good, they will think you worked all day on it. Simple ingredients, easy to bake and a great summer dessert! Top it with fresh whipped cream and additional berries for a wonderful dessert, or serve as is with a steaming cup of coffee or tea.

1/2 c. butter, room temperature
3/4 c. plus 1 T. sugar, divided
zest of 1 lemon, or 1 t. lemon
   extract
3 eggs

2 t. baking powder
1 c. plus 1 t. all-purpose flour,
   divided
1 c. favorite berries, stems
   removed

In a large bowl, blend butter and 3/4 cup sugar. Stir in lemon zest or extract. Add eggs, one at a time, beating after each egg. Add baking powder and one cup flour; stir until smooth. Pour batter into a greased 10" round cake pan or springform pan. Lightly dust berries with remaining flour. Scatter berries over batter and sprinkle with remaining sugar. Bake at 350 degrees for about 40 minutes, testing for doneness with a wooden toothpick. Makes 8 servings.

Make a handy mixture for greasing and flouring cake pans in one easy step. Combine 1/2 cup shortening, 1/2 cup vegetable oil and 1/2 cup all-purpose flour. Store in a covered container at room temperature.

Peaches & Cream

Brenda Hager
Nancy, KY

One of my husband's favorite desserts. I've had this recipe for so long, I can't remember where I first found it! It is easy to double for potlucks & carry-ins, just use a 13"x9" baking pan.

3/4 c. all-purpose flour
3-oz. pkg. cook & serve vanilla
   pudding mix
1 t. baking powder
1/2 t. salt
1 egg, beaten
1/2 c. milk

3 T. butter, softened
15-oz. can sliced peaches,
   drained and 3 T. juice
   reserved
1 T. sugar
1/2 t. cinnamon

In a bowl, combine flour, dry pudding mix, baking powder, salt, egg, milk and butter. Mix until smooth. Pour batter into a greased 9"x9" baking pan. Arrange peaches on top in a single layer. Spoon Filling over peaches and batter, spreading to within 1/2-inch of edge. Combine sugar and cinnamon; sprinkle over Filling. Bake at 350 degrees for 30 to 35 minutes. Makes 9 to 12 servings.

Filling:

8-oz. pkg. cream cheese,
   softened

1/2 c. sugar
3 T. reserved peach juice

Stir together all ingredients until smooth.

My advice to you is not to inquire why or whither,
but just enjoy your ice cream while it's on your plate.
– Thornton Wilder

Shrewsberry Cake

Megan Simpson
Smithsburg, MD

This recipe has been passed down in my father's family for many years. It is delicious with a hot cup of coffee. Sometimes I add fresh blueberries for a special treat.

1 c. butter, softened
3 c. sugar
3 eggs
3 c. all-purpose flour
1 t. baking powder

1 c. milk
1/2 c. applesauce
2 t. vanilla extract
Optional: 2 c. fresh blueberries

In a large bowl, beat butter and sugar with an electric mixer on medium speed. Add eggs, one at a time, beating for 3 to 5 minutes after each egg. Add remaining ingredients except blueberries and beat well. Fold in blueberries, if using. Transfer batter to a greased and sugared tube pan. Bake at 350 degrees for one hour and 15 minutes. Cool cake in pan for 15 minutes before removing. Makes 12 to 15 servings.

Before adding raisins, nuts, dried or fresh fruit to cake batter, toss them with a little flour...it keeps them from sinking to the bottom of the cake.

Swedish Yum Yum Muffins

Sue Troth
Alberta, Canada

This recipe was given to my by Pam, a woman I met at the University of Calgary married student residency. I am from New York State and she comes from Delaware. These are my favorite muffins, bar none.

1 c. milk	1 t. nutmeg
1 T. vinegar	1 t. ground cloves
2 c. all-purpose flour	1/2 c. shortening or oil
1 c. brown sugar, packed	1 egg, beaten
1 t. baking soda	Optional: 1 c. chopped walnuts
1 t. cinnamon	or pecans

Combine milk and vinegar in a cup; let stand several minutes. Meanwhile, in a large bowl, combine remaining ingredients except optional nuts. Add milk mixture and stir well. If desired, stir in nuts. Spoon batter into 18 greased or paper-lined muffin cups, filling 1/2 full. Bake at 350 degrees for 20 to 25 minutes. Makes 1-1/2 dozen muffins.

Cut the fat in muffins, brownies and other baked goods...
replace the oil with the same amount of applesauce,
puréed prunes or mashed pumpkin. Just pick a substitute
that blends well with the flavor of the recipe.

No-Mixer Banana Bread

Stephanie Turner
Meridian, ID

This easy banana bread is delicious. I like to use a combo of regular white flour and white whole-wheat flour, but you can use all of one or the other.

1/3 c. butter, melted
4 ripe bananas, mashed
3/4 c. sugar
1 egg, beaten
1 t. vanilla extract
Optional: 1/4 c. brown sugar,
    packed

Optional: 1/8 t. cinnamon
1 t. baking soda
1/8 t. salt
3/4 c. all-purpose flour
3/4 c. white whole-wheat flour

In a large bowl, stir butter into bananas. Stir in sugar, egg, vanilla and optional ingredients, if using. Add baking soda and salt; stir well. Add flours and stir until just combined. Pour batter into a greased 8"x4" loaf pan. Bake at 350 degrees for 50 to 60 minutes, until a wooden toothpick inserted in center of loaf tests clean. Place pan on a wire rack; cool completely before turning loaf out of pan. Makes one loaf.

For a fruity cream cheese spread, combine an 8-ounce package of softened cream cheese with 1/4 cup apricot or peach preserves; blend until smooth. So delicious on warm slices of quick bread.

Simple Fruit Cobbler

Linda Crandall
Pulaski, NY

When I was a Navy wife back in 1969, this dessert was very popular in our housing unit. It's still delicious and easy.

1/4 c. butter, sliced
3/4 c. all-purpose flour
1 c. sugar
1 t. baking powder
1/4 t. salt

3/4 c. milk
21-oz. can favorite fruit
 pie filling
Garnish: whipped cream or
 ice cream

In a 350-degree oven, melt butter in a oval 2-quart casserole dish. Tilt to coat dish; set aside. In a bowl, combine flour, sugar, baking powder and salt; stir in milk. Pour batter over melted butter; do not stir. Pour pie filling on top; again, do not stir. Bake at 350 degrees for 45 to 50 minutes, until golden. Serve warm, topped with a scoop of whipped cream or ice cream. Makes 8 servings.

Did you know...you can shake up whipped cream
in a Mason jar! Add 1/2 to one cup whipping cream to
a wide-mouth jar, close the lid tightly and shake
vigorously for one to two minutes.

Snowflake Pudding

Lisa Tessmer
Las Vegas, NV

Shared in memory of Patricia Erickson, Rosemont, MN. My mother loved this dessert! In my family, this wonderful dessert was only served on special occasions like birthdays and anniversaries.

1 c. sugar	1 t. vanilla extract
1 env. unflavored gelatin	2 c. whipping cream
1/2 t. salt	1-1/3 c. sweetened flaked
1-1/4 c. milk	coconut

In a heavy saucepan over medium heat, combine sugar, gelatin and salt. Add milk; cook and stir until gelatin dissolves. Remove from heat. Cover and chill; add vanilla. In a deep bowl, beat cream with an electric mixer on high speed until soft peaks form. Fold whipped cream and coconut into gelatin mixture. Spoon into a 1-1/2 quart bowl; cover and chill until firm. To serve, spoon pudding into dessert bowls; spoon Raspberry Sauce over top. Makes 6 to 8 servings.

Raspberry Sauce:

10-oz. pkg. frozen raspberries, thawed and crushed	2 t. cornstarch
	1/2 c. red currant jelly

In a saucepan, combine all ingredients. Bring to a boil over medium heat. Boil for one minute, until slightly thickened.

Stir up sweet memories... look through Grandma's recipe box and rediscover a long-forgotten favorite dessert recipe to share with your family.

Pecan-Pear Bake

Courtney Stultz
Columbus, KS

Desserts don't have to be loaded with added sugar. This recipe features natural, simple ingredients and it's delicious!

2 c. pears, cored and sliced
1 c. raisins
1/2 c. chopped pecans
1 t. vanilla extract

1 t. cinnamon
1/2 t. nutmeg
1/8 t. ground cloves

Combine all ingredients in a lightly greased one-quart casserole dish. Toss until fruits are coated with spices. Bake, uncovered, at 325 degrees for about 30 minutes, until bubbly and pears are soft. Makes 6 servings.

Keep a jar of pumpkin pie spice handy if you love to bake. A blend of cinnamon, ginger, nutmeg and cloves, it's delicious in sweet breads and muffins, not just pie!

Pan Apple Pie

Billie Jean Elliott
Woodsfield, OH

This recipe was given to me by my friend Emma. She is a wonderful cook and I love her recipes. I have served this many, many times. It is simple, easy and most of all it is super delicious!

8 to 10 McIntosh and Jonagold
   apples, peeled, cored
   and diced
2-1/2 c. sugar, divided
1 t. cinnamon
2 c. all-purpose flour

2 t. baking powder
1/2 t. salt
1 c. butter, softened
2 eggs, beaten
Optional: ice cream

Spray a 13"x9" baking pan with non-stick vegetable spray; add enough apples to fill pan. Mix 1/2 cup sugar and cinnamon; sprinkle half of mixture over apples. In a large bowl, combine flour, remaining sugar, baking powder and salt; mix well. Add butter to flour mixture and stir well; add eggs and stir well. Cover apples with flour mixture by spoonfuls. Sprinkle remaining cinnamon-sugar mixture over top. Bake, uncovered, at 350 degrees for 45 minutes. Serve hot or cold with ice cream, if desired. Makes 12 servings.

Create a heavenly glaze for any apple dessert. Melt together
1/2 cup butterscotch chips, 2 tablespoons butter and
2 tablespoons whipping cream over low heat.

Baked Oatmeal Blackberry Cobbler

Christina Mamula
Aliquippa, PA

My lightened-up version of an old favorite!

1 c. frozen blackberries
1 T. cornstarch
1 c. rolled oats, uncooked
1 c. almond milk or regular milk
1 c. unsweetened applesauce
2 t. cinnamon

1 T. sugar or calorie-free
    powdered sweetener
1 t. vanilla extract
Garnish: vanilla ice cream or
    frozen yogurt

Spray a 6-cup muffin tin with non-stick vegetable spray. In a small bowl, toss frozen blackberries with cornstarch until berries are coated. Divide the berries among muffin cups; set aside. In a separate bowl, combine remaining ingredients except garnish. Mix well and spoon over berries. Bake at 375 degrees for 20 minutes. Serve topped with a scoop of ice cream or frozen yogurt. Makes 6 servings.

Most fruit pies and cobblers can be frozen up to 4 months...
a terrific way to capture the flavor of summer–ripe fruit.
Cool after baking, then wrap in plastic wrap and aluminum
foil before freezing. To serve, thaw overnight in the
fridge and warm in the oven.

Sweet as Honey Apple Crisp

Wendy Ball
Battle Creek, MI

I had an overabundance of Honey Crisp apples and needed to do something with them. I was very short on sugar, but had the bright idea to make up the difference with honey. We were all pleasantly surprised at how delicious this turned out!

4 c. Honey Crisp or Braeburn
   apples, peeled, cored
   and sliced
1/4 c. sugar or calorie-free
   powdered sweetener
1/4 t. nutmeg
1 T. lemon juice

1/2 c. honey
1 c. all-purpose flour
1/2 c. light brown sugar, packed
1/2 t. kosher salt
1/2 c. cold butter, sliced
Optional: ice cream

Spray a 1-1/2 quart casserole dish with non-stick vegetable spray. Spread apples in dish; sprinkle with sugar or sweetener, nutmeg and lemon juice. Toss to coat apples; drizzle with honey. In a separate bowl, mix flour, brown sugar and salt. Cut in butter with 2 knives until mixture is crumbly; spread over apples. Bake, uncovered, at 375 degrees for 40 minutes, or until apples are tender and crust is crisp and golden. Serve topped with ice cream, if desired. Makes 4 to 6 servings.

At dessert time, set out whipped cream and shakers of cinnamon and cocoa for coffee drinkers. Tea drinkers will love a basket of special teas with honey and lemon slices.

Kiwi Cheesecake Dessert

Joyceann Dreibelbis
Wooster, OH

One day a nearby grocery store was giving out samples of this wonderful dessert. So I got the recipe and tried it myself. It is so easy to make. Put it together in less than 30 minutes, then chill...a great make-ahead dessert for busy days, potlucks and holidays.

1 c. butter, softened
1/2 c. powdered sugar
2 c. all-purpose flour
2/3 c. sugar

2 8-oz. pkgs. cream cheese, softened
2 t. vanilla extract

Mix butter, powdered sugar and flour in a bowl. Pat into a lightly greased 15"x10" jelly-roll pan. Bake at 350 degrees for 15 to 20 minutes, until golden; set aside to cool. In a separate bowl, blend sugar, cream cheese and vanilla; spread over cooled crust. Spread Kiwi Sauce over cream cheese layer. Cover and refrigerate for 4 hours to overnight. Cut into squares. Makes 10 to 12 servings.

Kiwi Sauce:

3/4 c. plus 1/3 c. cold water, divided
1/2 c. sugar

2 T. cornstarch
5 to 6 kiwi fruit, peeled and cubed

Bring 3/4 cup water to a boil in a small saucepan over medium heat. Meanwhile, dissolve sugar and cornstarch in remaining water. Stir sugar mixture into boiling water; boil for one minute, stirring constantly. Remove from heat; cool completely. Stir in kiwi fruit.

Peel kiwi fruit in a jiffy. Slice off both ends, then stand the kiwi on one end and slice off strips of peel from top to bottom.

Lemon Sponge Pie

Shirley Condy
Plainview, NY

Yum! This pie is a favorite of my family and there is never a crumb left.

2 T. butter, softened
1 c. sugar
3 eggs, separated
3 T. all-purpose flour

1/2 t. salt
zest and juice of 1 lemon
1-1/2 c. milk, warmed
9-inch pie crust

In a bowl, blend butter and sugar. Add egg yolks; beat well. Add flour, salt, lemon zest and juice. Stir in milk; set aside. In a separate deep bowl, with an electric mixer on high speed, beat egg whites on high speed until stiff peaks form. Fold egg whites into butter mixture. Pour into unbaked pie crust. Bake at 325 degrees for 45 to 50 minutes. Cool completely before slicing. Makes 8 to 10 servings.

Keep ingredients on hand for a quick-fix dessert. A real life-saver whenever you receive a last-minute potluck invitation or your child announces, "Mom, there's a bake sale...tomorrow!"

Old-Fashioned Nectarine Pie

Sheila Murray
Tehachapi, CA

A scrumptious fresh fruit pie...real comfort!

2 9-inch pie crusts, divided
1/3 c. all-purpose flour
1/2 c. sugar
1/2 t. cinnamon
1/4 t. salt
1 t. lemon zest

6 to 8 nectarines, pitted
　and sliced
1/4 c. butter, diced
Garnish: small amounts milk,
　sugar

Place one crust in a 9" pie plate; set aside. In a large bowl, combine flour, sugar, cinnamon, salt and lemon zest. Add nectarines; mix lightly. Spoon nectarine mixture into pie crust; dot with butter. Add remaining crust; pinch to seal edges and cut 4 slits for steam vents. Brush crust with milk and sprinkle with sugar. Bake at 400 degrees for 45 minutes, or until crust is golden and juice begins to bubble. Cool before slicing. Makes 6 to 8 servings.

When making double-crust pies, use a mini cookie cutter
to cut vents out of the top crust. The cut-out pieces
can be "glued" around the edge of the crust with
beaten egg white...so pretty!

Plum–Pear Puff Dessert

Joanne Mauseth
Reno, NV

My daughter Amy and I came up with this delicious treat one Sunday afternoon. It is simple, fast and delicious. Try it with apples instead of pears and add a little cinnamon to taste. Any favorite jam can be used too.

1 sheet frozen puff pastry,
   about 14 by 12 inches
1/4 c. plum jam
1 to 2 pears, cored and sliced

1-1/2 T. brown sugar,
   packed
1 egg, beaten
1 T. water

Thaw puff pastry at room temperature for about 30 minutes. On a lightly floured surface, roll puff pastry into a 17"x11" rectangle. Lay pastry across a lightly greased baking sheet. Spread jam over half of the pastry, starting on one short edge. Arrange pear slices in a single layer to cover jam; sprinkle with brown sugar. Fold over other half of pastry to cover pears; roll edges to seal. Whisk together egg and water; brush over pastry. With a knife, lightly score pastry to mark desired servings; do not cut through. Bake at 400 degrees for 18 to 20 minutes, until golden. Serve warm or cold. Makes 8 servings.

If your baked dessert didn't turn out quite right, layer it with whipped cream in a parfait glass and give it a fancy name. It will still be scrumptious... and nobody will know the difference!

Peanut Butter Freezer Pie

Diana Krol
Nickerson, KS

My daughter Emily requested this pie for her 25th birthday dinner. It's become a family favorite since then. This pie is very rich, so be sure to cut it into small slices. Yum!

8-oz. pkg. cream cheese,
    softened
2 T. milk
2/3 c. sugar
1/2 c. creamy peanut butter
8-oz. container frozen whipped
    topping, thawed and divided

3/4 c. mini semi-sweet
    chocolate chips
9-inch chocolate cookie crumb
    crust
Optional: additional whipped
    topping, chocolate chips

In a bowl, beat together cream cheese, milk and sugar. Stir in peanut butter and 1/2 cup whipped topping. Fold in remaining topping and chocolate chips. Spoon filling into crust; cover and freeze. Remove from freezer 20 minutes before serving time. Garnish, if desired. Makes 8 to 10 servings.

It's easy to make your own crumb crust. Mix 1-1/2 cups fine graham cracker or cookie crumbs, 1/4 cup sugar and 1/2 cup melted butter; press into a pie plate. Chill for 20 minutes, or bake at 350 degrees for 10 minutes.

Chocolate Cobbler

Linda Roper
Pine Mountain, GA

This delicious made-from-scratch dessert goes fast...
you may want to make two, just in case!

1 c. all-purpose flour	3 T. butter, softened
3/4 c. sugar	1 t. vanilla extract
2 T. baking cocoa	1-1/2 c. hot water
1/2 c. milk	Garnish: whipped cream

In a bowl, mix all ingredients except hot water and garnish. Pour into a lightly greased 13"x9" glass baking pan. Sprinkle with Topping; carefully pour hot water over all. Bake at 350 degrees for 40 minutes. Serve warm, topped with whipped cream. Makes 10 to 12 servings.

Topping:

1/2 c. brown sugar, packed	1/4 c. baking cocoa
1/2 c. sugar	

Mix together all ingredients in a small bowl.

Coffee adds a rich taste to chocolate recipes. Just substitute an equal amount of brewed coffee for the milk or water called for in cake, cookie or brownie recipes.

Index

Index

Index